C000136437

I
NEVER
WAS A
COWBOY

I NEVER WAS A COWBOY

FELIX RAINOSEK

PALMETTO
PUBLISHING
Charleston, SC
www.PalmettoPublishing.com

Copyright © 2024 by Felix Rainosek

All rights reserved

No portion of this book may be reproduced, stored
in a retrieval system, or transmitted in any form
by any means–electronic, mechanical, photocopy,
recording, or other–except for brief quotations
in printed reviews, without prior permission of
the author.

Paperback ISBN: 979-8-8229-4822-8

TABLE OF CONTENTS

Foreword

CHAPTER 1: CHILDHOOD

CHAPTER 2: THE MILITARY

CHAPTER 3: CIVILIAN LIFE

FOREWORD

I grew up around cowboys, real cowboys with horses and herds of cattle. I found out quickly that I wasn't cut out to live that life. It wasn't that I didn't like that life or that kind of work. I just learned early in life, and it continued into my adulthood, that a horse hasn't been born from which I cannot fall. I have literally fallen off every horse I have ever been on. Now I don't just fall off like a drunken idiot; I get tossed off or, as the cowboys say, bucked off. I never knew why every horse I ever looked in the eye wanted to toss me on my ass, but it did. They say horses know who is riding them, whether they know what they are doing or if they are scared. Horses knew I wouldn't last two jumps, that's for sure. Even a Shetland pony tore me up. I was probably eight or nine years old, and that should have told me at once that I was not a cowboy, and I could have saved myself some pain and scars over a few years.

My dad had lots of horses, and when I say lots, it wasn't a herd of them; it was a lot of horses coming and going. He was a horse trader in the real sense of the word. So this gave me many opportunities to show my prowess of not being able to ride. Even in later years riding at my good friend Chuck's house, I had the dubious reputation of being able to be thrown from his horse and never spill a drop of my beer. It has been said far and wide that, while I am falling from a horse, my arm will contort and break the laws of physics to keep my drink upright. So, I have that superpower going for me. It is embarrassing, really. I am a die-hard Dallas Cowboys fan—live and die with them—but mostly die lately. But I never was a cowboy.

I authored this book with the intent in mind to bring to light the interesting people I have known during my lifetime and the interesting, odd, and funny things they do. They have made my life much more colorful and have made many memories to smile and laugh at. I also included some of the more interesting highlights of my life. I don't think I am so interesting, but my life, my choices were formed by my interaction with other people. If you get far enough in this book, you'll find that the discipline I developed in the army helped me in my recovery from brain cancer, and that same discipline was a direct result of my interaction with other people and our shared experiences. This writing can sometimes take on a serious note as we know that life is not always like a carefree life lived inside a sitcom, but I tried to keep everything light and humorous. I think if I had a superpower besides not spilling my beer while falling, it would be that I can find the humor in almost every person and every situation.

Another superpower is that I am a big people watcher. People will tell you all about themselves and never say a word. When I do happen to strike up a conversation, if I wait five minutes, a stranger will tell me all about themselves so I can fill in the blanks. Once in a great while, someone comes along in my life that does the same thing. My brother-in-law Jack is such a person. He is aware of everything and everyone around him. I think he could tell you the color of the shirt of the person driving the car behind him. It is even more fun to interrupt his people watching. He is a professional people watcher, and I consider myself a novice compared to him, but I do more than most do. He could author a book about perfectly good strangers and the strange things they do and say.

I read somewhere lately that a school librarian wore the same dress for forty days in a row before anyone in the school, student, or faculty, noticed or at least said anything. I am not sure how many days it would take me to notice but I can usually spot that somebody has owned the same shirt for a few years. Maybe I should have been an investigator or a police officer. Maybe I should have been a clown in Barnum and Bailey. As you read about the people in my life and my life in general, you could produce a lengthy list of possible vocations I should have taken advantage of. Again, I tried to keep it light, hopefully not only showing the humorous side of people but also their good side. Everyone I write about and mention by name is someone that is or has been close to me, a good friend, and I cherish their memories forever. Face it:, you are funny and interesting and people need to know it.

I left so many people and stories out of this book. My faith and the miracles that I have seen happen to me and others could be another book. Maybe it will someday. I don't speak a whole lot about my family when I was young because my memory and my recollection of particular stories don't always jive with others' memories when I ask them for clarification. A child's memories are usually bigger than they may be for someone else.

One such colorful person I have known my whole life who helped shape my people watching is my brother-in-law Jerome. He is quite the character, but when I was a child, he always made me feel at ease, and I listened to everything he would say. He was my fishing buddy while I grew up and my golfing buddy on my visits after I left home. He had a colorful vernacular, to say the least. One day we were talking about bugs, and he was telling us how this bug does this or that. My wife, Pam, asked if he was sure. He said, "Hell yes. I studied ANT-tomology." He is like a lot of folks where I come from in the fact that he speaks two languages, and growing up, English was not necessarily his first—Czech was. He has a lot of home cures passed down through generations and other odd fixes for various things, many more than I can tell here. He's pure Texan and can regale you with tales, and whether they are tall or not is debatable sometimes, but he is a wise man and a people watcher too. He should author a book.

I just wrote about two brothers-in-law in my family, Jack on my wife's side and my sister Jocelyn's husband Jerome, in the preface, and I haven't even started on the book yet. Turn the page, but first, I am curious. Can you stay atop a horse?

CHILDHOOD

My childhood, now that I've been looking back on it, was probably a lot like many others' who grew up in the country. Food came from what you grew or raised. I guess we didn't have much money, but I never knew it. I always ate until I was full and complained about having T-bone steaks again. We had fried chicken every Sunday, and sometimes Dad would come home with some BBQ from Sweet Home. A local man cooked BBQ every Sunday, and it was the best I ever had. He called his homemade sauce Comeback sauce—you eat some, and you'll always come back for sure, and he was right. But Mom always made a couple of fried chickens that came from our yearly chicken processing day. Nobody fries chicken quite the same way that Mom did. She made batter for the chicken with lots of eggs, so it was very eggy. It was good and the only reference to fried chicken I had for years. She also made banana pudding. It had a layer of bananas, vanilla wafers, and then some pudding, and then layered it all over again. I often offered to help make it because it was like an art form to place the pieces just so inside the bowl. When it was fresh, it was great, but as soon as the vanilla wafers would soak up too much moisture from the pudding, it was terrible, although we all ate it either way because I don't think we threw out too much food.

I was always bigger than the other kids my age. My dad was well over six feet, they say six feet four inches, and always around 240 pounds by the time I came around. I thought for sure since I was bigger than my peers that I would be his size as well. It didn't happen, but that didn't stop me from enjoying my strength and speed advantage over the other kids competing in sports for a little while. I have brothers, Elvis and Emil, and two sisters, Jocelyn and Wanda, all of whom are older than me. I looked up to my brothers and followed them as much as they would let me, although there was a definite age difference. My sisters were my babysitters, or at least my middle sister, Wanda, was. I remember my middle brother, Emil, and I used to pester her while she tried to watch her TV program, and she would chase us out of the house and put the latch on the screen door to keep us out. Emil would take a piece of wire and stick it through the screen on the door, and we would be inside again to pester Wanda. It wasn't like she sat around and looked at the TV all day—she had house-work, cooking, and chores to do. She worked hard, we just didn't realize it at the time. This was the one time during the day that she could take a break. I think the show was called *Dark Shadows*. One time Wanda chased us as we ran out into the barnyard, and there was a little stack of fence stays by the gate of the yard. A fence stay is a heavy gauged wire that was bent over in two and twisted. You put the open-ended side of the stay over the top barbed wire in a fence and twisted the stay down for a while until the end reached the next wire, in which you inserted it and on down to the next and the next. The idea was to keep all the wires the same distance apart from each other even when the wire wasn't very tight. Anyway, they looked like spears, and Wanda grabbed one and threw it at us and nailed Emil in the head with it. As most head injuries do, he bled badly, although I always thought he was more frightened by the blood than the actual cut. We had to call my older sister, Jocelyn, to come home and clean him up with a water hose. He survived, but I don't think Wanda got to finish *Dark Shadows* that day.

We didn't hide too much of this type of monkey business from Mom, but we had to from Dad. Dad drank too much and was happy one minute and scream-ing mad the next. I think these days he would have been called bipolar, but that wasn't a thing back then. Now I admit that, to me as a small child, he was scary, kept me on edge most of the time; I was always wary of him and avoided him most of the time. That is the worst I will say about my dad, because I have also learned that he worked extremely hard for his family, building barbed-wire fences and pole barns, hauling hay, and even butchering calves and processing them for people. He tried a little bit of everything, it seems now. I have since learned that he did the best he could. If there were meds back then to help with his bipolar problems, everything might have been all right. I watched my brothers like a hawk to figure out what I could get away with at home, but I did some stupid stuff when I was little. One day I went out to my dad's pickup and found a box of contact pills—you know, the cold medicine in capsule form with colored beads inside of them. I took them out, broke the capsules, and poured out the little beads. I was smart enough to know not to eat them but not smart enough to leave them alone. My dad later went out to get his cold meds in the truck and found the package empty. Somebody remembered me being in the pickup and was a big tattletale. I was summoned and then took my dad to the truck and showed him the little beads all over the ground that he hadn't seen before on his visit to retrieve them. He asked me if I ate any of them, and I told him no. He was so relieved, but I got a good ass whipping for that one.

Another time my mom was making sauerkraut. She had a table set up in the barn and was filling jars full of cabbage and whatever else it was that made that awful stuff. I ran into the barn, and I guess I saw the table was empty on one side, so I jumped up on the empty side, and the table collapsed under me, and the jars slid down the table, crashing down on top of me onto the floor breaking many jars. I don't really remember any ass whipping, but I sure deserved one. My mom was more worried about a barefoot boy getting up around all that broken glass.

The Dallas Cowboys were our favorite team, and I was Roger Staubach. I didn't have the patience or the stamina to sit the amount of time it took to watch an actual game on TV on Sunday afternoons, so I went outside with my football and my imagination and played football in the barnyard. We had a clear spot that was probably ten yard wide and thirty yards long, although in my mind it was a big football field. There was a chicken coop on the left and a hackberry tree with a basketball goal on the right. Those targets took a beating, especially the coop. I took the snap, took a few steps drop, and threw the ball at the coop or the tree. I used the tree sparingly, because that old hackberry had rough bark, and it would scuff up my football if it hit too many times. Our laying hens were allowed to roam during the day, so the door to the coop was open. If I threw the ball through the door, it would be a touchdown. If I hit either side of the coop, it was just a completion, and if I threw it over the top or hit the ground first, it was incomplete. Sometimes, since I was Roger Dodger, Captain Comeback, and Captain America all rolled into one, I would have to scramble. I'd play outside from the second quarter until I was tired or curious to see what was happening in the game inside on the TV. I'd go back in and quiz my brothers on what happened during the game, and then I'd watch Roger bring the Cowboys back from a most certain loss and earn a glorious Dallas Cowboy victory—the same glorious victory that I had engineered in the barnyard. I suppose some of the wins were easy, and surely they lost sometimes, but I really only remember the comebacks, and there were a lot of them.

My mom bought me a football book, one that predicted the coming year and showed all the stats from the past year of all the football teams. It had little write-ups about certain star players on each team along with rosters and the colleges each player attended. It was all new to me, and I became a stat freak, and I still am today. I would borrow the family calculator and come up with more stats than the book provided. I quickly saw through my calculations that the best quarterbacks with the biggest yards per catch were always in the playoffs. That book opened a new life for me. I wrote in that book all kinds of different stats and how they affected each player or team. During the season I would get my hands on the *Victoria Advocate* newspaper and comb through the sports pages to get the box scores and stats. I didn't know it at the time, but I guess I was in training to be a bookie. The trouble was that somebody else came up with those same ideas, and a lot of them have been used over the years. When watching a game, they showed these stats. I always thought that I missed my calling. I should be looking up the stats for some TV network or team. Like I said, I'm still a stat and trend freak. I play a lot of fantasy football today using those same principles. Although you can change the name of your team daily, mine is either America's Team or Stats, Facts, and Figures, a nickname I picked up with friends in the league who give me crap about always talking about stats and trends.

GRANDMA

When I was little, before school age, my grandma from my mom's side was my babysitter. She loved me, and I loved her a lot. She could barely get around due to a bad hip, and she could hardly see a thing, but she still was an excellent babysitter. She liked *The Price Is Right* TV show. It was the only show she watched that I know of. She would sit in her rocking chair next to her TV and didn't bother looking at it because she couldn't see it, and I would sit on the edge of her bed right next to her and answer any questions she had about the show and the prizes. I was Bob Barker's play-by-play announcer. After the show she would turn the TV off because she didn't want to waste her electricity. She was green before it was cool to be green, because she never wasted anything. She would make mashed potatoes for lunch, and then the next day she would fry the leftovers with butter, onions, and lots of black pepper. She toasted them to perfection with little brown flakes throughout the potatoes. For someone who couldn't see what she was doing, she sure was a chef when it came to potatoes.

She had a big vegetable garden and a huge flower garden all around her house. It was like walking through an enchanted flower forest for a little guy like me. We would go out in the vegetable garden every day and go down a row picking out weeds and come back again. When the vegetables were ready to pick, I would go pick them. I especially remember picking cucumbers because you had to pick them with a chopping hoe. I would take the hoe and rake the leaves of the cucumber plant looking for copperhead snakes, and if I found one, I would wrap him up with the hoe and toss him out and give him a good chopping. We had to do that at home as well, although my siblings would usually do the snake handling. I know what you're thinking. What's a little kid less than school age doing having to deal with poisonous snakes? That's the way it was back then. I hear folks these days say, "Aw, poor kid can't do this or that. They're too little." I cry bull crap. Kids can do a lot more than you think if they're taught correctly and given a chance. Back to Grandma.

She lived across the pasture from us about a football field away. When I was very little, first-memories little like three or four, she would walk over to our house, but after a while it was decided that I would walk to hers because she had that bad hip and found it hard to cross over fences anymore, plus her eyesight was getting worse. At my house we played dominoes, and I have a sneaking suspicion that she would always let me win. Somehow when it was my turn to start the game, I always had the double five and scored ten points. Some, like my brothers and sisters, say that Grandma let me win a little too much and made me a spoiled child who didn't like to lose at anything, but I'm not sure about all that nonsense. I loved my grandma then, and I love her even more now thinking about her and the times we had.

I loved my grandparents on my dad's side as well. Grandma Rainosek made wonderful kolaches, a Czech dessert. They were so good they were also breakfast, lunch, and supper as well. I remember making home-made ice cream on my grandparents' porch, taking turns churning the ice cream by hand. My cousins would be there for a big party that happened about once a month. My grandpa would roll his own cigarettes, and I remember how odd the smoke smelled. It wasn't bad but wasn't good either. I think that's the reason I never smoked in my life. But Grandpa would take us fishing and would be full of helpful hints on how to catch a fish. They seemed to work. He and I would walk through his corn field and look for raccoon tracks. We would find them and see which way they turned, this way and that way, and he could get a good grasp of how many were out there judging by the size and the number of tracks in all the different directions. He never took me out at night to hunt them, however.

We would help my grandparents plant their potato garden. Once, when I was teenager, I was there to help Dad plant potatoes. Like most folks back then of their age, they watched the moon phases to tell them the best time to do virtually anything. We hooked up old Sammie the jackass to a plow to begin the dirt work, and my grandma stepped out on the back step and hollered at us, "It's not the time to plant potatoes!" She was basing this on the current phase of the moon.

My dad hollered back at his mother, "I plant potatoes when I got time to plant potatoes!"

She muttered, "You won't get much yield, but do what you want to do," and went back inside. Even she knew there wasn't much use in arguing with Dad.

One Sunday afternoon—I was about five—Grandma R. was charged with babysitting me. I was showing her how I could hit a baseball over the roof of the house. She was impressed as much as a grandma could show. I got a little overconfident and started to hit the ball over the house right in front of our living room window. That window was just begging to get hit, but I was too good at tossing the ball into the air, and I hit a perfect hit over the roof. Grandma warned me repeatedly not to do that, but I didn't listen, and after a while, *CRASH*!!! The ball went right through the window. Grandma gave me a good talking to, and she cleaned up the glass. My goose was cooked good, and I mentally prepared for my ass beating when my parents came back home. They finally came home, and my dad was having a fit while I was being covert and hiding. My grandma talked him down, assured him that it was an accident, and he let me live. I have been grateful to Grandma ever since.

My grandparents and a lot of our neighbors were of Czech heritage. It was and still is a way of life for that area of Texas. Everybody could speak the language, but that stopped in my generation. Mom and Dad would speak Czech to each other when they didn't want us to know what they were saying. Music was a big part of my growing up. Grandpa played the fiddle; his brother, my great-uncle Emil, played the guitar, and my uncle from my mom's side of the family, Uncle Linwood, played the guitar and sang very well. Our neighbor Raymond, who lived down the road, could play the accordion and harmonized very well with Uncle Linwood. He could sing very high. When they all got together, it was a concert for us. They played all the polka classics, and we all sang along. We sang in Czech sometimes, which meant I sang along in gibberish, but it was such great fun. My favorites were the "Red Wine Polka" and

"No Beer in Heaven." Another was "Apples, Peaches, Pumpkin Pie." I would stare at the guitars and Grandpa's fiddle. Grandpa tried to give me lessons a time or two, but he said I was too severely left-handed to learn to play right-handed, and he was not changing his strings around for lessons. When Charlie Daniels says in his song "Devil Went Down to Georgia," "When the devil pulled the bow across the strings, it made an evil hiss," he wasn't talking about the devil, he was talking about me. I never had any more opportunities for music lessons, and that is the one thing I really wish I had done, and I regret not begging for guitar lessons or something. We had a little electric organ that I learned to play. It had a songbook that had numbers in it instead of musical notes. My great-uncle Victor would come over to visit, and I would open a window while my parents and he would sit outside in the evening and listen to me play. I was good, but pianos today don't have numbers.

At the same time, when were at home, we listened to the radio, and my brothers spent their money on eight-track tapes. I really liked the Beatles, Credence Clearwater Revival, Chicago, Amazing Rhythm Aces, Steppenwolf, the Guess Who, Bread, Bachman Turner Overdrive, Thin Lizzy, and some others I can't recall the names of. I grew up smack dab in the middle of the outlaw movement with Waylon Jennings and Willie Nelson as well.

That old hackberry tree in the barnyard had a basketball goal on it. There was a fence post close by, and I put my radio on top of it and listened to 55 KTSA out of San Antonio. My radio was shaped like a Texas Longhorns helmet. It sat on a lot of fence posts all over the place, including in the garden. I played basketball while listening to it for hours. I was a fairly good shot, but I never bothered learning how to dribble properly, mostly because my ball was rarely aired up enough to do so. Once again, I used my imagination to play a game. I scored a hundred points a lot of the times in the games in my mind, and my mom kept me supplied with nine-volt batteries.

BETSY AND THE FARM ANIMALS

We always had animals around of some kind, and they always served a purpose, which was usually to eat. We had a milk cow named Betsy that kept us in plenty of milk supply. Pigs, sheep, an occasional goat or two, and horses were always around. My dad, whose nickname was Cowboy, was an original horse trader, so I could never expect to see the same horse around two days in a row. We had a mare named Angel that was a constant at home, but that was about it.

I milked Betsy for a lot of years both morning and evening. We sold some milk sometimes to folks in town, but mostly we had plenty of milk ourselves and drank it with every meal. Betsy would have a calf every year, and I would take a bucketful and would let the calf have the rest. When the time came to wean the calf off her, we had to get another calf to drink half of her bag. Getting Betsy to accept a strange calf was difficult, but I figured out a way to do it easily. Betsy was allowed to roam the barnyard all day, and we kept the calf in a pen. I'd put some feed in a bunk in an adjacent pen to the calf, and Betsy was always happy to come in and eat while I milked a bucket full. When I was done, I would open the gate to the adjacent pen and let the calf in. That calf, who just minutes before was extremely jealous of me and the milk I extracted, was now grateful for me opening the gate. Betsy was cross at first. She would kick the crap out of the new calf, and I'd have to holler at her and stay in the pen to try to get her to behave, but she wasn't too scared of me. But one day I noticed a bull whip sitting somewhere doing nothing, so I brought it over. The confines inside the pen were a little too small for the use of a bull whip, so I stood outside the pen with the bull whip in hand. Betsy had this routine: she ate, she turned to look back at this strange calf and then proceeded to kick the crap out of it. So I learned that, as I stood there with the bull whip and watched Betsy eat, when she turned to look at the calf, I would twirl the bullwhip over my head and *CRACKKKK*!! Oh no, I wouldn't hit poor Betsy—I just cracked the whip outside the pen. Betsy was so startled that she stuck her nose into the wall and just stood there like a stone cow. After a minute she would start to take a bite or two. She'd stand there chewing and then look back at the calf again and CRACKKKKK!!! Her nose went straight into the wall again and stood perfectly still. After a week or so of this, she accepted the calf as her own, and I didn't have to employ the whip anymore. I used this method on Betsy to get her to accept many orphan calves. If a boy could be proud of outthinking a cow, it was me.

I was feeding all the animals one evening. We had a pigpen that had a trough right next to a wooden fence that was about chest high to me, and I would lean over the top and dump out the mud or dirt that was in the trough. I picked up a five-gallon bucket filled with slop and poured it out into the now-clean trough for the pigs to eat. My belly would balance on the top board as I poured it out with pigs coming running, pushing, and shoving. I avoided them all. I got done and turned around, and a buck sheep was staring at me from five yards away. This buck had horns that wrapped around his head back down to his jaw. We had a history; words were spoken before, and I think he held a grudge as he remembered every one of them. I stood there with my back to the wall, looking at the buck with nowhere to go. The pigs were behind me gorging on the slop I had put in, and I did not want to take any chances of getting in with their hungry mouths and trying to make my way through a muddy pen. Suddenly the buck came charging at me and hit me directly in the stomach/chest area, and I dropped to the ground like a wet rag. He knocked the air out of me for the next several minutes. Thankfully that one charge was enough for him, and he trotted off victoriously. I had watched him very carefully before this incident, and now I had to watch him even closer.

We all rode horses, but I think Emil was probably the best rider of all of us. He even took to trying to break horses. My dad built a roping arena and put up lights, and lots of folks came over to rope calves. The problem was that calves figured out that they were going to be roped after a couple of times through the chute. One time I rode Angel to rope a calf. I remember that I roped my calf, probably my first ever. I was riding along the fence line to get to the gate at the front of the arena to get out of the way. The next calf was let out of the chute, and a kid named Joey, a few years older than I—he was around Emil's age, was taking his turn. I was watching the action and walking Angel back, and the calf turned forty-five degrees and started to run right at me. I stayed the course. The calf got right up on me and decided to turn and go where he was supposed to go, but Joey did not. His eyes were on the calf, swinging his loop over his head and concentrating on the calf and not me. His running horse collided with Angel, who was walking, and we got knocked over. I took a tumble with Angel, and she jumped right back up like nothing happened with me still in the saddle. Hey! I stayed on a horse!! I thought I should be busted up, broken hip, ribs, back, head, something. The gate opened, and I walked out with Angel like nothing happened with all the guys standing around laughing at the proceedings. My mom usually let us have our fun, but that was the one time she came running from the house and said— no, demanded, screamed, hollered, commanded—that my fun was over. I got off that horse and never got on one again that day. I realized later that she was saving me from being surrounded by a bunch of people who have had too much alcohol, and my safety was not first and foremost on their minds. It was probably a good decision by Mom. As far as wrecks go, I've had lots of wrecks where I could have and should have been busted up bad but never even got a broken nail. Horses and motorcycles, I never met one I couldn't fall off .

One day my sister Wanda saddled a Shetland pony that had come from somewhere. She took her turn riding it, and I waited for my turn. I thought, "What could possibly go wrong with such a little horse?" I may have been eight or nine at the time, so I was as small a person as the horse was as small a horse. Wanda finally relinquished the reins, and I got up in the saddle. Usually when I rode a horse, my feet didn't reach the stirrups, but this time they did. I'm guessing we had a kid saddle; I just didn't get to use it much. I took off at a lope in the little pasture behind our house, and as luck would have it, the girt strap came loose, and the saddle completely flipped over under the horse's belly. To make matters worse, my feet were stuck in the stirrups, and for once in my life I stayed atop—I mean below—the saddle. My head dragged the ground for a while until somehow I was able to get my feet loose. That poor pony just skipped over the top of me, and I was lucky I was not hurt once again.

SWEET HOME SCHOOL

I started school in the first grade at Sweet Home School. It was and still is a little-house-on-the-prairie type of school in a small community. We had four kids in my class counting me. My sister Jocelyn worked there as a secretary or a paraprofessional—I'm not sure what she was doing there, but it was nice to have her there. Every day in the afternoon, we had the chance to buy an ice cream bar of some kind for a quarter. I never had any money, so I would run into her office and would beg her for a quarter every day. She always gave me a quarter, and I always got a Dreamsicle, the vanilla ice cream bar on a stick with an orange crunchy cover on it. I loved those things and Jocelyn bought one for me every day. The best thing is that, even today, I am the only one who remembers this; she doesn't remember this at all, so this excuses me from having to pay her back. Nine months of school, twenty days a month. That comes out to about forty-five dollars' worth of Dreamsicles.

MISS MARTHA

I had the same teacher for six straight years, from first grade through sixth grade, Miss Martha. I didn't always get along with her, but she did prove that she loved her students and cared about their education. Miss Martha never got married, she had a few acres and a few cows, and she taught at Sweet Home School for so many years that she taught all my siblings as well. It was a running joke for all of us in school, but every year when Miss Martha had a birthday, she was sixty-three years old. I swear she told us that for six years running, but she looked more like eighty. I don't mean to sound mean about her; God rest her soul. I suppose she didn't want us to know her age, and besides, as kids we didn't know at the time, but it was considered rude to ask a lady's age. She was a bit aggravating to me, but at the same time, I had a soft spot in my heart for her. She was the only one outside my family that thought I had the potential to do anything I wanted to do. She told me so many times. She'd constantly remind my mom as well every time their paths crossed. Even when I moved on to Yoakum High School, she always asked my mom about me when they saw each other in town.

This next story is something I had nothing to do with. I was always involved with pranks in school, but this one was on the girls in my class. At some point our class got bigger by 20 percent when one person was added, Monica. On the south side of the school, we had a big porch with a wash sink. I'm not sure why that sink was out there other than to splash your head with water during recess on a hot day. The fourth, fifth, and sixth grade classroom was inside the building right next to the sink with the only thing separating them being a wall and a long line of windows that served as the only air conditioning we had. Miss Martha would sometimes take her book for whatever class she was holding, go over to a bookshelf on the south wall, and lean up against it to try to get some air herself. For some reason my classmates Monica and June were sent outside to do something on the porch. They had a bucket or wash tub, something that held a large amount of water, and they filled it up. They noticed Miss Martha was leaning on the bookshelf at the time, so they thought it was a clever idea to throw a bucket of water through the screen of the window and splash Miss Martha. The girls tried to run away and back into the schoolhouse so they wouldn't be caught. Miss Martha let out her patented saying she had when someone was in trouble, and I heard it often. "*Aalllll riggghttttt!*" The girls were screwed, and there was no getting out of this. It was the oddest thing that I have ever seen in my eight years in Sweet Home School and I was not even involved. I don't remember what their punishment was, but I'm sure it was severe. Those girls grew up to be kind of crazy anyway. I'm not sure where they are today, but I'm quite sure if I ever ran into them, they would probably throw a bucket of water at me too, just for old time's sake.

My memory is not necessarily good from that period. I called my mom, and her recollection of a story was different from mine. I remember that we had games against other schools in softball and volleyball, and we always won, except for one that I can remember. We played coed softball and volleyball.

We also had a 4-H track meet every year, and we always won that as a team. In the fifth and sixth grade, I won all my events. Remember, at the time I was bigger and faster than everyone else. In the seventh grade, however, a new kid showed up at one of the schools who was a fast son of a gun, and he beat me fair and square in the sprints. All my life, even as a kid I have fought the battle of the bulge. I guess my eating habits weren't very good, and I got a little on the heavy side sometimes. I knew to be able to win in the eighth grade I had to train hard. There were no coaches, only our principal who did the paperwork and drove the bus to get there. I began to run and train hard for the eighth grade track meet. I was self-trained, but I was driven. My events were the 60-, 100- and 220-yard dashes, the softball throw, and the four-by-one-hundred relay. Five events were all we were allowed to compete in, and I won every time in the fifth and sixth grade but faced defeat in the seventh grade in a couple of the sprints. I did train hard, running all the time at recess instead of playing games. Grandma's domino game teaching of not being able to lose came in handy because, when we finally got to the track meet, I smoked everyone by a large margin. The county extension agent who put the meet on said I should run backward to give everyone else a chance. I know what you're thinking. That guy's grandma did not do him a great service. Maybe so, but what I did learn is the value of training and preparation for things in life. Looking back, I'm not particularly proud of the blue ribbons—it was just a kids' track meet. But I am proud of the way I saw something I wanted, saw the obstacle in my path, and prepared hard to beat it. I've used that principle all my life.

HIGH SCHOOL: RONNIE'S COWBOY EXPERIENCE

In high school my best friend, Ronnie, was and still is a great guy and is loyal to a fault. He really wanted to be a cowboy and, like many in Texas, dressed the part very well. He was a year younger than me, and when he came to high school, we hit it off well. I decided I would take him out and give him the opportunity to be a cowboy and go riding. I took him to a pasture my dad leased out in Hope, Texas. Hope wasn't a town by any means, but it did have a sign. It was just a couple of houses, so I guess if you were in Hope, you had hope, but if you weren't in Hope, you were out of hope.

Back to the story. My favorite family horse, Angel, was out there along with a new horse my dad had just bought from somewhere, and it seemed nice enough in the fact that it didn't run off like a wild banshee when we walked up to him, even in a pasture. We put bridles and saddles on them, and I told Ronnie that he was going to ride Angel because she was gentle and, besides, I didn't know anything about this other horse, and if anyone was going to get killed by this horse, it should be the owner's son and not the owner's son's friend. Ronnie said no, that Angel was too tall and the other horse was shorter, so he would prefer to ride the shorter horse. So I thought, what the hell, why not? The horse was easy to catch and easy to saddle—it was likely this horse was fine.

My brother Emil happened to have some chaps in the pickup, and Ronnie put them on, and it turned out to be a good idea. Anyway, I'm jumping ahead. We climbed up in the saddles and took off walking to go check the cows. The cows were in an open field near one of the gates. We had to walk through a line of trees to get to that part of the pasture. We were having a fun time talking, being cowboys, and coming up on the cows before too long when suddenly Ronnie and his horse turned on a dime and started to go back. I looked at Ronnie as he was turning, and he was smiling at me. They trotted back to the tree line and disappeared into the trees. I thought that Ronnie wanted to go off on his own, and, besides, I had cattle to count and check.

I counted the cattle and looked back at the trees with much curiosity. Ronnie and this new horse were nowhere in sight. I started to run back, wondering where they had gone. After a few seconds, they emerged from the trees, Ronnie on foot with the reins in his hands. I got to Ronnie and asked, "Where did you go?"

Ronnie said, "This horse just turned on his own and ran back to the trees on his own."

I asked, "Why didn't you say something? I looked at you, and all you did was smile at me."

Ronnie replied, "The horse turned so fast and caught me off guard that my nuts got smashed against the horn of the saddle and I was gritting my teeth, dammit—I wasn't smiling."

Now Ronnie is famous. He's the only guy who can smile when he gets hit in the nuts.

As it wound up, the horse had run under a limb that was too low for Ronnie to duck under, and he got knocked off the horse and landed in or around a wild rose bush or something thorny. Good thing he put on those chaps. The horse just stopped and stood there once Ronnie was off his back. He walked the horse out from the trees, and that's where I found him.

Dad always said not to let a horse have its way then quit riding unless you got your leg or back broken. The horse needs to know who the boss is, and you have got to show it as much before the saddle comes off. I decided that I needed to ride this horse and give it a lesson in who's in charge—a wasted lesson, because the horse already knew. But I walked him into our little corn patch, probably an acre or two fenced-off spot. I had picked a lot of corn by hand out of that patch in my day, but that day the ground was bare. I decided to run this horse and show it who's boss.

I took off at the gate and ran down to the corner and reined the horse left down the line. We got to the next corner, and I reined another left to go down the length of the field. The horse thought he should be done already and turned to go back to the pickup, which was parked near the gate. I reined right, and he wasn't having any of it. I tried to stop, and he didn't want to do that either. We were getting close to the gate, which wasn't a real gate, a gate you can buy at the local farm and ranch store. This was what we called a gap, one of the barbwire fences where you take a small fence post and pull it tight and put a loop of wire over the top of the post to close it.

I had a runaway horse who really wanted to take me back to the pickup and have me load up the saddle I was riding on. I was pulling up this horse's head so high trying to stop, it could've given me a weather report. I decided to let him have his head down so he could see the gap was closed and he should stop. This horse was blind as a bat, because it was not slowing down heading to this gap. I didn't know what to prepare for, whether he was going to run through this fence or whether he was going to try to jump. I had to guess, and I guessed wrong. I got prepared to jump, which is to be loose in the hips and ride with the flow of the jump. At the last second, this horse decided to put on the brakes and skidded on all four legs.

My loose hips and I were totally unprepared to stop, and I went on its neck, or its neck went up on me. Through careful consideration, the horse decided that it had made a mistake and decided to jump after all. I never was a cowboy, but I kind of knew that I was in a real cowboy predicament. The horse was not a good jumper, or to be fair to the horse, it was, but just on the wrong foot to do so, but it tore down the gap. In my own terrible situation, I fell from this horse and landed flat on my back on the hard, sunbaked Texas soil.

It knocked all the air out of me. I couldn't breathe. Ronne was right there to help but not sure what to do, and neither was I. I finally sat up and was able to get a little air into me. The horse did run off about thirty yards or so away and had stopped to stare back at us. He was ahead two-zero in knocking want-to-be cowboys off his back.

We conceded; the horse had won. We walked over, grabbed the reins, walked back to the truck, and unsaddled him and Angel. I hoped Angel didn't get any crazy ideas from what she witnessed that day. I still felt terrible from having the breath knocked out of me and was getting thirsty from all this excitement, but we came unprepared. There was a cooler in the back of Emil's truck, and I was hoping that it had something in it and hopefully it was still cold. I opened the cooler, and I was wrong again. It had one can of Pearl beer in there, and it was hotter than hell.

I had seen Chuck Norris drink hot Pearl beer in the movie *Lone Wolf McQuade* and thought I could too. I popped open that hot beer can with gusto and downed it on the spot. I thought lying on the ground unable to breathe was a bad feeling, but this was worse. I had downed beers before, but never a hot one while I had lung problems like I did.

OK, let's get this out of the way. Yes, I was only sixteen, and yes, I wasn't supposed to be drinking alcoholic beverages. You must realize this was Texas, and this was in the 1980s, which to Czech country folks like us, could've been 1880. Beer was a way of life.

I recovered and took off driving down the road to Jocelyn and Jerome's house. She would have some cold tea or at least some ice water. She hooked both of us up with something cold to drink. I wonder how many times she saved me in some way or another. Anyway, we made our way back home to unload our saddles for the day and get Ronnie back home. In the next day or so, I told my dad about this horse's antics, but after finding out which bridle we used, he said I used one with a jigger bit, and the bit was pinching the horse's tongue and driving it crazy. I never was a cowboy, but if a jigger bit pinches a horse's tongue, why do we have a jigger bit? Once again, that horse didn't last long enough around the place to find out if that was true or not. I really didn't care to find out.

My dad was a horse trader. I'm sure I'll repeat this fact several times. He bought and sold so many horses and cows so often and so fast that he often didn't even have to unload them from the trailer. I'd come home from school and find a horse in the back of the trailer that was hooked up to his pickup. I'd look it over and went about my business. My dad would drive off and come back late with an empty trailer. I asked him several times when I could tell he was in a talking mood what had happened to that horse or cow that was in the trailer earlier in the afternoon. He always said, for example, he bought the horse for $700 in the morning and sold it for $750 in the afternoon. He never took a loss in all the times I asked him, or at least he claimed not to.

THE GRAND THEATER

I went to Sweet Home School in, naturally, Sweet Home, Texas. Hey, it's there—google it. After the eighth grade, I had to go to Yoakum to attend high school. There wasn't much to do in a small town like Yoakum, but the one thing there was to do was go to the movies at the Grand Theater. It was a Friday night tradition for my friends and me. I don't remember every movie, but we saw a lot of early eighties scary movies like *Wolfen* and *The Howling*. I remember taking my neighbor Dottie to see the movie *Stripes*. It's no wonder that both Dottie and I joined the army, and she stayed and retired years later. But getting back to the Grand, it was a shrine to most Yoakumites. The first movie I saw at the Grand was *True Grit* with John Wayne. When Maddie fell into the snake pit, I sat there with my hands over my eyes scared to death.

Perhaps the most unusual movie was on a Halloween night in 1981 or 1982. I don't remember the name of the movie, but it was absolutely disgusting. It had burning bodies and people hanging on crosses. It was a terrible movie. What was worse was that our party that consisted of Rickie, Robbie, Lisa, Mary, Barbara, and me were in the front row due to the movie being close to a sellout. I'm not sure we made it to the end of the movie, but when we left we went to a local haunted house.

The haunted house was conveniently located in an open area next to the railroad tracks, kitty-corner from MooMoo's convenience store. That's what's great about Texas. It has some of the most unusual things, names, history, more than any other state. But back to the story. I knew before we went in that it was a bad idea. A kid, I'd guess about twelve, came running out of the exit with a monster chasing him. Poor kid. He grew up with a lot of things to work out in his head. We paid our money, and we went in. They should have paid us. It didn't take long for someone to recognize one or all of us and give us a bit of extra attention. It was attention I didn't care to have. Someone fired up a chain saw, and I decided to haul ass through the house like that twelve-year-old boy. Hey, chivalry is dead at this point, and it was killed by a murderous, bloody fiend with a chain saw. I was wearing my favorite terry cloth shirt that night. I wore my favorite terry cloth shirt every Monday, Wednesday, and Friday. For some reason I thought laying it on the floor on Tuesday and Thursday aired it out. OK. I'm just kidding now.

Back to the story. One of the girls decided to hitch a ride by grabbing onto the back of my shirt. I'm sure that instead of hitching a ride, it was more like clinging to a leash of a starving Saint Bernard dog trying to get to a meal. When I got out, my poor terry cloth shirt was down to the knees in the back. The front of my shirt bore a slightly chubby six-pack. Someone still owes me a shirt, and hopefully they read this, and then each will feel compelled to get me one.

CITY MEAT MARKET

In my sophomore year, I took a job at City Meat Market. At the market we processed calves, had a meat window counter, and made and smoked sausage. The front of the place was a small grocery store, and the back was a BBQ restaurant. Ninety-nine percent of what I did there was bone out meat and make various types of sausage. We made a beef wiener that was delicious. I always thought that if marketed correctly, that wiener could have made millions. The BBQ, however, was less than desirable, but people came in to eat, so what do I know? The Market was the first place I fully understood that people were different. Until that time the only adults I mingled with were my parents and other family members, my parents' friends, and maybe a neighbor and teachers, but that's about it. And even with that, I rarely talked to adults, although I listened to them when I was around them. They were all Czech and mostly the same, and that's the majority of what I saw. But at the Market, we had all Caucasian people except Mr. Vera, who was the sausage expert and the best knife sharpener I have ever seen. We had Lenert, who was old and worked part-time and only in the mornings helping make sausage and bone bull meat. The rest of the employees were the owner and the owner's family, except for a few colorful others. Leslie was the owner, Louie the owner's brother—but also a minority owner, I always thought. Paul was Lesley's son. And then there was Marvin. Marvin worked part-time because he also drove an ambulance and was probably an EMT as well as a volunteer fireman. He should have been a nice guy, but he was a rough customer instead. He wasn't very big but wore Levi's boot-cut jeans and big, giant cowboy boots. He only had one eye, and the other was fake and often looking slightly off from the other. He also wore black-framed glasses. He walked with a John Wayne sideways slide. We never knew what his schedule was—he just showed up. Vera would be making sausage and standing at the cylinder pumping meat into the casings. Lenert would stand next to Vera and would be tying sausage or twisting wienies. I would be standing next to Lenert doing the same and hanging the sausage or wienies on a smoking rack. Suddenly the back door would wildly swing open, and Marvin would slide in. He'd holler, "G'morning all you Mexicans, bohemians, and square-headed dutchmen."

Lenert, who had a squeaky, heavy German accent and resembled Sergeant Schultz from *Hogan's Heroes* TV show, would ask him, "Which one are you?" Marvin never answered.

We had an old, half-drunk Mexican guy who started the BBQ every morning. Marvin would always give him crap and remind him that he was a Mexican. One day I heard the old guy reply, "I know I'm a Mexican—you don't have to tell me." Oh sure, I'm from the south and I've heard every kind of derogatory name one can say to another about their race, creed, or color. But I never heard it spoken with such disdain as I heard it when Marvin said it. As I got some experience working there and even got to work side by side with Marvin, which scared me to death at first, I realized that he was just joking—he just had a way of saying it that made me think he was serious and mad. He would get Lenert to scream sometimes because he would give him so much crap about anything. Marvin knew how to get people fired up. It didn't really work on Vera. Vera was a nice fellow, close to retirement age, and very soft spoken. He was really like a Mexican version of Mr. Miyagi from *Karate Kid*. He surely thought I was stupid, because I never could learn how to sharpen a knife like he could even though he showed me how several times.

As Lenert showed up even less and less, my buddy Ronnie got hired. We made a lot of sausages with Vera. We got another part-timer, Kat, who I would come to learn had worked there on and off for years. Kat was a Mexican, about five foot one, who had a belly that protruded almost as far as his arms. His big belly was as hard as a rock. He was very strong and didn't take much crap from anybody but sure could dish it out. For some reason a guy named Randy was hired.

Randy was about six foot three, could hardly learn to do anything, cussed more than any person I had ever known. Kat would pick on this guy, and Randy would get mad very easily. Randy would get so mad that he would start screaming cuss words, and after he was done saying every cuss word he knew, he would turn around and spout them all over again. Sometimes he would say one back to back. Ronnie and I could never understand the reasoning behind that and would often repeat him, but he thought it was funny when we did it. We didn't pick on him, although we did kind of play with him at times. I think Ronnie was first to really feel sorry for him, because Randy had a cleft lip and didn't enunciate his words very well, even the cuss words. His eyes were crossed as well. I think Ronnie and I were probably his best friends. We didn't think he had much except family outside of work.

One day Kat was at the processing table and Randy was at the sausage table. The folks at those tables were close enough to talk but couldn't see each other, because they were placed at a right angle, and working at either table meant you were mostly back to back. While Kat mostly picked on Randy, today Randy was on Kat. It entertained Ronnie and me. Kat walked up behind Randy, reached between Randy's legs, and grabbed his testicles and gave a good squeeze. Randy gave a mighty howl as his legs went out from under him and he fell to the floor with Kat still clutching onto his poor gonads.

Kat asked him if he was going to quit whatever it was that Randy was doing or saying. Randy cried out loud, "*Yeeeeeee*!!!" About that time, we had a little old lady that worked the cash register by the door, and for some reason she came walking in the back door of the processing room. She saw Randy on the floor, Kat's hand between Randy's legs, and Randy letting out moans and groans that sounded worse than any wounded animal. She walked through there extremely fast and never uttered a word and, to my memory, never came in the processing room again. Kat finally let go, and it took some time for Randy to recover. Luckily Leslie and Louie, owners and brothers, did not come in during this time. It was a great place to work for a young man. The only problem was working in that cooler all day during the summer and them coming outside in the hot Texas heat at quitting time was almost unbearable.

UNCLE LOUIE

We had our share of characters working at City Meat Market, and Uncle Louie was one of them. His brother Leslie was the official boss and owner of the place, and maybe Louie had a share of the ownership, because he sure acted like it. Also, he wasn't my real uncle; he was Leslie's kids' uncle, and they were always around, especially Paul, who was a highly skilled meat cutter in his own right. But Ronnie and I took to calling him Uncle Louie as well.

Uncle Louie usually had something to say about everything, and it was usually something a young idiot like me should listen to. He used to tell stories about his time in World War II working in the field artillery. Oh yeah, that's the MOS I chose as well...hmm, wonder why? He always said war was fun if you were advancing. Nobody was shooting at you, and you got them on the run. But war was hell if you were retreating. You're still trying to shoot rounds while hauling ass trying not to get caught or bombed to pieces. He made it sound fun even though it wasn't. Leslie was in the war as well, and they told of the day when they ran into each other in a town after months of not seeing each other or even knowing if the other was alive. Leslie was in the infantry and didn't tell many stories about the war, but Louie sounded like he had a wonderful time.

Uncle Louie was also quick to put you in your place. Many times he heard the childish rambling from Ronnie and me, and he would tell us in no uncertain terms that we knew nothing and that he forgot more about the subject we were talking about than we knew.

He was tough on customers sometimes as well. A guy came in one day and wanted round steaks, a whole leg's worth. Knowing meat like I do now, I cannot fathom what he wanted with them. Chicken fried steaks, maybe? He asked Uncle Louie for the biggest round we had, and Louie went in the back, found one, and put it on the scale, and it weighed forty-four pounds. He went back out and told the guy. We were in the processing room boning out bull meat, so we really didn't know what was going on at the counter, but it wound up that the guy wanted to see the scale. The door flew open, Uncle Louie and this guy came in and looked at the scale, and Louie told him, "See? Forty-four pounds." The guy said he'd take it. Uncle Louie said, "You will not!!!" I don't remember the exact words, but suffice it to say that, when Uncle Louie told you the weight of something on the scale in the processing room, you had better believe him and not even think that Uncle Louie was even a tad dishonest. The guy didn't get any round steaks that day from us.

Like a lot of guys, Uncle Louie liked his beer. We closed at six, and at five he would go down to the Diamon Shamrock station down the street and buy a six-pack of Budweiser. After a while he would give me a five-dollar bill and send me to go get it for him. The legal buying age was eighteen at the time, and I was sixteen to seventeen years old. I always looked older than my age, so I could get away with it. Our cleaning guy, we called Pancho Frijoles, was sick and couldn't come to work for a while. Ronnie and I stayed over to clean the processing room for that time. After everyone left we would take our own five dollars and get us a six-pack while we were working. When Pancho came back to work, when we got off at six, we would go to Quick and Easy and buy a six-pack and drink it riding around town. There was a nice lady who worked in Quick and Easy. She sold that beer to me without a question, but I suppose one day we talked about school or something and she asked me how old I was. I told her the truth, sixteen, and put my cash on the counter. She said, "OK," and took the cash. Funny how cash answered the question for me. A good lesson I learned early in life, cash talks.

I played sports in school and was good at them, but I hurt my right shoulder sliding into second base head-first and couldn't move it like it was supposed to. That put a stop to being good at athletics. Our doctor said it was OK and would get better. It did, but it took a long time, and there were still ways I couldn't move it even thirty years later. As it wound up, I had a torn ligament. I finally found out when I tore two more and required surgery. I loved baseball, and that shoulder really put an end to my career for the most part because if you can't raise your glove hand over your head, you're not very good at baseball. I have to say here, though, that through all my life playing sports of one kind or another, my mom was supportive and rarely missed a game if she was in the same country. Even in my military life she came up to Kansas to watch me play in a military softball tournament.

I enjoyed high school and had some teachers I thought were wonderful and some not so wonderful. I guess the ones I thought weren't so wonderful probably thought that I wasn't a wonderful student either. The wonderful teachers I remember were Mrs. Zaruba, an English teacher who also directed all the plays, and Mrs. Parr, the typing teacher. Now you wouldn't think a rough-and-tumble guy like me would like typing, but it is a skill that I mastered well enough that it has helped me in life more times than I care to count. This book wouldn't have happened if it weren't for that typing class. I only signed up for typing class because I thought the class would be full of girls. I was right, but Mrs. Parr taught me well, and I was interested in typing. Mr. Thibodaux was a math teacher. Originally from Louisiana, he was an interesting character who sold little packets of crackers for twenty cents at his desk. He owned a racehorse named Blue Jet King, and he always kept us abreast of the horse races. I had an algebra teacher I really did not like. I didn't understand him at all and had to work to get by. And most of my classmates had the same problem. He just explained things backward it seemed. He was one of those we said was so smart that he was dumb.

It my fault I got involved, but one day some of us guys got into a HORSE game in class. The game was throwing wads of paper at a trash can and the person behind you had to make the same shot or get a letter—just like basketball. It was agreed that the person who exited the game first had to take licks from the teacher's paddle that equaled the number of total shots he missed. There were five or six guys involved. How could an athlete like me lose? Well, I did, and that total came to twenty-three licks from a paddle. It was all my fault, and I really didn't think he would go through with it, but he did. Luckily for me the first three were hard, the next seventeen were just little taps, but the last three—and already having stinging butt cheeks didn't help—he laid into me really hard. I lost fair and square, but now after all these years I wonder if that teacher might have enjoyed that a little too much.

There were lots of fun times in school, but a little side note. Remember I told the story earlier about a movie and a haunted house. Through the magic of Facebook, I asked some of the people involved about it, and there are discrepancies. Some don't remember it the same, not all agree who was there, and one person doesn't remember it at all. I don't know what's wrong with all these people's memories. Why am I the only one who remembers exactly what happened? That's why I'm stopping here with the school stories. I'm not sure that I am 100 percent correct in my recollection, and if the story involves others, I don't want to risk telling it wrong. The stories I have told, however, are very vivid in my mind, and I feel confident enough to tell them, although some may not remember it quite the same way. With that said, I graduated and joined the army.

THE MILITARY

ARRIVING

I joined the US Army in the spring of 1983 on the delayed entry program. There were supposed to be advantages to the delayed entry program, but they didn't benefit me except to give me time to realize how bad I screwed up by joining. I admit I had my days of apprehension, but I didn't want to hang around after high school, and I didn't want to work in the oil fields like my brothers. I thought I wanted to see the world. My dad thought it was a mistake as well. He was a typical country guy who had his share of superstitions. I had a great-uncle, Felix, who died in France in WWII, and my dad thought that I was following in his footsteps for sure. All I wanted was the bonus of $8,000 that came for signing up with the field artillery. But still, the more time I had to think about it, the more I thought I wanted to stay, because I feared the unknown. Where would I go? What's going to happen to me?

My brother-in-law Robert was a tremendously great help to me during that delayed period. He explained virtually everything that was going to happen during basic training and beyond. The information he provided was indeed valuable, because when I got to my basic training station, Fort Sill, Oklahoma, I knew what was going to happen before it happened. The other new recruits quickly gave me the nickname of Radar, the name of the character in the TV show *M*A*S*H* who knew what his commander was going to say before he said it. I liked it. It made me the go-to guy for questions.

We were busy getting our uniforms, shots, mighty fine haircuts, learning how to march and stand at attention, nothing too strenuous. Let me get this one point out about mighty fine haircuts. You spend a day with the guys, and you recognize guys by the color of their hair or their hair style. You get to talk with some fellow and think, "This guy is great; he can be a friend of mine." You get in line and get that buzz haircut and *wham*! Where did that guy go? We all looked the same. You had to start all over finding that guy or, like me, just give up on it. Now back to the story.

Some of the guys thought this indoctrination isn't so bad, but I warned them we were not at basic training yet. After two or three days, a bus showed up, and we all loaded up on the bus. I made the mistake of sitting in the back seat on the driver's side with my two fully loaded duffle bags. My newfound friend Melvin from Houston was sitting on the other side with his duffle bags. We took off down the road. A little Black man with a Smokey the Bear hat on his head was standing at the front of the bus. Occasionally he turned and looked at us with a crazed look in his eyes and his teeth bared—not a smile, or a sneer, just a look like he was having trouble breathing and his teeth were too big for his mouth. The bus came to a stop in the middle of a bunch of two-story buildings. That drill sergeant, Drill Sergeant Jones was his official name we found out later, turned to us and said, "You got sixty seconds to get off this bus, and fifty-nine of them are done gone!" Lots of screaming by DS Jones and our new DS Ramirez led up into a frenzy of activity to get off the bus. Once again, taking some advice from Robert, don't be last. I got into a shoving match with Melvin—I was pushing him and my duffle bags in each hand and he was pushing me. I wonder what we looked like, two kids pushing each other with duffle bags trying to get in the aisle of the bus. I won, but it didn't matter. Outside the bus was total chaos. We dumped the bags on the ground never to see one of them again until after graduation.

My alter ego, Radar, knew what was happening most of the time, but I was not a weather forecaster. I, along with all my fellow recruits, was dumb enough to report for basic training during July in Oklahoma, where the temperatures can climb as high as 114 degrees. We were in a line and told to walk very fast, not run, down a sidewalk. Suddenly all the drill sergeants were screaming at us. One would come at me and scream, "Walk fast!" I was walking as fast as I could, so I started into a trot. "Do not run!" would be the next command screamed in my face. I began to walk as fast as I could. "Walk faster!" came another scream to the ear. Well, what the hell do you want? Luckily Robert once again saved me from further problems because I knew that sooner or later the DS was going to ignore me and jump on somebody else's back about their gait.

At one place in the sidewalk journey, we had to stop, take our possessions out of our pockets, hold them high above our heads, and get sprayed down with a water hose to alleviate the heat effects. I guess it worked, but I didn't like walking very fast, not running, in wet boots.

We entered a building with chairs and sat down and received instructions on how to do everything. We learned to say, "Drill Sergeant, yes, Drill Sergeant!" We learned other important info that was meant to keep us from getting chewed out and do endless push-ups, something that we were just learning about that very day. DS Jones came up to me and asked my name. I answered correctly, "Drill Sergeant Jones, my name is Private Felix Rainosek, Drill Sergeant Jones!" Of course, he could see my last name on the name tag on my brand-new uniform.

"Ranasappy," he replied. "Ranasappy, you look like an insurance salesman. Do you sell insurance?"

"Drill Sergeant Jones, no, Drill Sergeant Jones!" I was trying very hard to remember the new protocol for speaking to my DS that I had just learned precious minutes before. I had passed, and he moved on to the next unlucky guy to test his memory.

I was assigned to Alpha Battery. As time went on, I met and became friends with lots of guys from all over the United States and Puerto Rico. I began to see that cultures were different as well as language and slang, but we were all in this together. Our barracks was a two-story building, and all the Black guys in Alpha Battery took up residence on the bottom floor, except for one white guy, and all the white guys and others were on the top floor except for one Black guy. I could see that segregation was alive and well in 1983, and I often wondered why the drill sergeants didn't make us split up a little more. Hmmm…whatever—I got more to say on this later.

I already had my nickname, and sooner or later everyone got a nickname. There was Gomer, Country, Lando from Orlando, and Stinky McNasty, who got his nickname because he didn't want to be naked in the shower with all the "homos." We finally threw his nasty ass in the shower with his uniform on and dumped a box of laundry detergent on top of him. If one didn't get a nickname, they were simply called by their last name. My favorite guy was Opie, named because he looked like the spitting image of Opie from *The Andy Griffith Show*. Robert was his proper name, a good ol' boy from Oklahoma. He was and still is to this day a very colorful guy. There was no telling what he might say and very nice and giving. He was a groomsman at my wedding a few years later.

My goodness, lots of stories from basic training—where to start? I have to say from the start that at this time of my life, only thirteen weeks in, I learned more about human nature than I had in the first eighteen years of life. There was a lot of what seemed like physical torture, being pushed to limits I didn't know I could reach, but also watching others reach theirs and seeing them overcome or break down. Outside our barracks we had a five-bench bleacher where we would sit in the evening time, shine our boots and our brass buckles, and hear stories of what life was like in Georgia, or North Carolina, or Pennsylvania, places I thought were a million miles away but suddenly were in front of me. The stories those bleachers could tell. One of the lessons Robert taught me was you will mess up sooner or later and the DS will get on to you and stay on you to see if you will break. Don't take it personally; it's just a test of your strength and will. It's not as bad if you know it will happen like I did. Stories to come with my struggles with DS Jones later.

COLEMAN

One day we were sitting in the bleachers, shining our boots, and the lone Black guy who bunked upstairs, Coleman was his name, said something that DS Jones heard from his office window upstairs. The following happened.

DS Jones shouted out of his upstairs window for Coleman to come up there right quick and in a hurry. Coleman ran through the open front door (no air conditioning here) and ran upstairs. DS Jones screamed at him for at least thirty seconds and then tells him to go downstairs and give him twenty.

Now a little information about push-ups and talking to drill sergeants. When doing push-ups you addressed the drill sergeant, then after each one you shouted the number of the push-up you just completed, and then the words "drill sergeant" again. You were never given more than twenty to do at a time. You think this is easy, but after the 20th, you had to ask for permission to speak. You were either given or denied permission. Given permission to speak, you then asked for permission to recover, which also you were either given permission or not. Now back to the story. Coleman ran down the stairs and quickly jumped down in the lean-and-rest position and began to count out. "Drill Sergeant, one, Drill Sergeant. Drill Sergeant, two, Drill Sergeant," until he reached twenty.

Coleman, down in the lean-and-rest position: "Drill Sergeant Jones, Private Coleman asks for permission to speak, Drill Sergeant Jones."

DS Jones: "Hell no!"

Coleman just stayed there. After a minute or so, Coleman asked again: "Drill Sergeant Jones, Private Coleman asks for permission to speak, Drill Sergeant Jones."

DS Jones: "Speak, maggot!"

Coleman: "Drill Sergeant Jones, Private Coleman asks for permission to recover, Drill Sergeant Jones."

DS Jones: "Hell no! Stay down there, maggot."

Coleman was in a bit of a fix. After a while he asked again and was given permission to both speak and recover, but this was far from over. DS Jones again called him upstairs and chewed him out some more, told him to go down and do twenty push-ups. Poor Coleman went through the procedure again and was told no to both being able to speak and to recover. Soon after what seemed like several minutes, he was given permission to do both and called up again. That poor soul was chewed out again. Now my fellow recruits and I had our heads down and silent, working on our boots or buckles. Looking at us you would think we were sitting there and Coleman and Drill Sergeant Jones were ghosts we couldn't see, and we had no idea what was going on. But we did, and we were all on the edge of our seats, and I, along with others, was beginning to feel sorry for Coleman—not sorry enough to butt in, however. He was on his own. But when you are in that front lean-and-rest position too long, your arms start to shake and your hips start to drag making your body into a banana shape. You will be told to straighten up, in a slightly different way, however. I think the words used were, "Get your dick out of the dirt!" Oh my, don't dare fall and give out unless you are hurt. A fellow broke his arm while in the lean and rest a little too long. Opie and I liked the guy, but he didn't come back.

Anyway, back to Coleman. Coleman ran back down the stairs and fell the last few steps, got back up, and started to knock out twenty more. I think he was on his set of eighty or one hundred push-ups. He asked for permission to speak. Of course he was told no. Coleman was shaking badly. Of course, my head was down concentrating on my boots, but my eyes were up watching Coleman, and so were everyone else's. We didn't want to get caught looking too interested in the proceedings, lest we may become a participant in the proceedings.

Finally Coleman cried out, and I mean cried in a most pitiful, high-pitched, shrill voice: "Drill Sergeant *Jooooonnnnneeeessss*! Private Coleman asks for permission to *speeeeaaaakkkkk*! Drill Sergeant Jones!" Coleman was actually crying.

DS Jones: "Speak, maggot!"

Coleman: "Drill Sergeant *Jooooonnnnneeeessss*! Private Coleman asks for permission to *recooooovvvvveeeeerrrr*! Drill Sergeant Jonesssss!" I must admit Coleman sounded worse than a dying cat in a hailstorm.

DS Jones allowed Coleman to recover and told him not to do whatever it was or say whatever he said again.

Now Coleman was in the lean-and-rest position with his head facing us and away from the barracks and DS Jones's office. After being given permission to recover, Coleman jumped up to his feet and gave us a giant smile like he just got away with the slickest trick in the world! He fooled us all. I thought he was near death, and he was just acting like he was crying.

My favorite movie about baseball is *The Sandlot*. When Squints pretends to be a drowning victim and Wendy Peppercorn gives him mouth-to-mouth, only to find out he's faking. When she looks at his chest and Squints has that big, wide, toothy grin on his face, I automatically think of Coleman.

LANDO'S AIM

Basic training was eight weeks long, but we had the pleasure of stretching it out to thirteen weeks because

AIT (Advanced Individual Training) was five weeks long, and we stayed in our barracks with our drill sergeants during AIT as well.

During basic there are many basic skills and basic weapons you must master, and the grenade launcher was one such weapon. It was mounted on the bottom of an M16 rifle and was a lot of fun to shoot but not very accurate. You pointed it at an arch and pulled the trigger and hoped to throw it out there close to your target. You really couldn't aim it. The cool thing was that you could watch the grenade all the way, because it was lobbed out there like a softball pitch, but faster. What made matters worse, however, is that to fire it you had to be in a prone position, which is lying face down, propped up on your elbows, with the butt of the rifle planted firmly against your chest so your pectoral muscle takes the brunt of the recoil. If you were a normal-size guy like me, it was manageable, but for little guys like Lando, who may have been five foot four and a whole 120 pounds if that much, it was near impossible.

We were at the range and learning to operate the grenade launcher. We all shot a few paint rounds, which were rounds not filled with explosives, but paint instead. We had various targets to shoot at; junk vehicles like Jeeps and tanks were mostly what was down range. Hitting anything was hard, but like the old saying goes, close only counts in horseshoes and hand grenades, or in this case grenade launchers. If you had a few rounds to shoot, you could adjust your fire to finally paint a target. Those of us who had either shot already or were waiting to take our turn stood behind the few who were shooting. We didn't have many grenade launchers out there, so we had to wait our turn and, of course, some good-natured near-silent heckling was going on for those who missed badly. It got to be Lando's turn.

He got down in the prone position and struggled mightily to hold the weapon up to his chest. Not only was Lando small, but he also wasn't very strong. He writhed and wiggled on his elbows, the muzzle of the M16 waving way too much to be very effective. His legs were together, then separated, then back together, as if trying to make a snow angel. Lando could not find a comfortable spot. As if on cue, DS Jones came walking up behind Lando and watched the struggles that Lando was having. Lando was trying to aim at a tank about a hundred or so yards away. Lando was lying there, M16 still wavering, legs spread apart, and DS Jones got into a stance behind Lando as if to kick a field goal and said, "Lando, you better land that grenade through that hatch on the side of the tank, or I'm going to kick you square in the nuts."

He stood there patiently waiting. The tank had an open bay on the side of it, not noticeably big and certainly a target too small for a grenade launcher. We stood half snickering and half worried about Lando. We knew DS Jones was not going to kick him, or would he? Lando was obviously struggling, and this new threat had not helped his nervousness. *Thump*! Lando fired the grenade launcher. We all watched its projection toward the target. It looked good—certainly it would be close enough to do damage to a real tank with a real grenade. We all thought it may even hit the tank. The closer it got the better it looked until *swish*! Like Jordan putting a basketball through the hoop, nothing but net, the grenade went through the hatch without hitting a side. DS Jones watched it, saw it, got out of his kicking stance, and simply walked away without a word. It's the only time I can remember DS Jones being completely speechless. When Lando recovered from his position, he was speechless too. He admitted he tried to look over his shoulder and saw DS Jones behind him and really thought DS Jones was going to kick him square in the nuts.

SLEEPING WITH MY M16

Like I said earlier, DS Jones was going to get you sooner or later whether you did anything wrong or not. DS Jones got onto me several times but never any worse than the morning after he had stolen my M16. Our platoon was out on bivouac, which means camping, military style. We were out there for a week doing all kinds of activities, some of which are other stories I will share. But this story is the story of DS Jones getting me good.

At the beginning of basic training, you are issued gear, and one of the pieces of gear is a half tent, stakes for one side, and a tent rope. You take your half of the tent and snap it to someone else's half tent; your stakes hold up one end, your buddy's stakes hold up the other, and you tie the whole thing down with your tent ropes. Really a smart idea, but you really wanted to be meticulous about who your tent mate was. You sure didn't want Stinky McNasty, but after a couple of days out there, we were all stinky. We were all issued sleeping bags as well, but in Oklahoma in July, the bag was just a makeshift mattress to lie on. I don't remember who my tent mate was, but he was a good one who didn't seem to bother my sleeping habits which were akin to being dead.

After a day of activities, I was tired. It came time to sleep, and I lay down on my sleeping bag with my trusty M16 laying by my side. I slept well. I was awakened in the early morning by someone on guard duty. I began to get dressed and ready for the day, but my M16 was gone from my side. What the hell??? So much for being a trusty rifle.

I asked around, and naturally my M16 had seemingly fallen off the face of the earth. I knew what I had to do. I found DS Jones standing by a large tree with an M16 slung over his shoulder. The problem therein was that DS Jones didn't carry a trusty M16 like the rest of us. I walked up to him expecting the worst. I said,

"DS Jones, Private Rainosek asks for permission to speak, DS Jones." He let me speak right off, because I assume he was really interested in what it was that I was going to say.

"DS Jones, Private Rainosek wants to report that he is missing his M16 from his tent this morning, DS Jones."

DS Jones went off. He informed me in no uncertain terms that luckily it was him that had my M16 and not some Russian who wanted nothing more than to slit my throat and take my weapon. I didn't think it would help to remind him that if an actual Russian were on Fort Sill, I would likely sleep with a loaded weapon. He handed me my M16 and promptly ordered me to drop and grab a piece of real estate, which meant to get down in the lean-and-rest position. So I slung my M16 over my wrist to keep it out of the dirt and mentally prepared to do some push-ups and stay down there awhile.

I did my push-ups, counting off each one like I was supposed to. All the while DS Jones was bent over screaming at me about not securing my M16. I asked for permission to speak but naturally was denied. He continued to scream and berate me. When he finished his tirade, I asked again to speak. I don't remember how many times I had to ask to speak and to recover; it was a number larger than two. When he finally let me recover, he called me to attention and berated me some more. He then ordered me to hold my M16 out away from my body. I did this until I could no longer hold it up. Arms aching and out of breath, I was called out for being weak. He ordered me to get in the position of attention. He then ordered me to do a left face, which I executed.

"Get down and give me twenty." DS Jones thought he afforded me enough time at attention to get some rest into my weary arms, but he was wrong. I struggled and counted out push-ups only to be denied the right to speak. Sooner or later, he allowed me to speak and recover, gave me the riot act once again, and ordered me to hold out my M16 away from my body one more time. Three more times I had to do a left face, a complete circle, and get down and do push-ups. Three more times I tried to hold the weapon out away from my body; the amount of time I was able to hold it out there was dwindling with each passing order to do it. I was determined not to give up or give in. I had seen several of my fellow recruits already break down, want to fight, scream, argue, lie down and cry, only to be marched off never to be seen again. This was not happening to me. To this day I wonder why he pushed me so hard like this. Yes, he had done it to others with great success in breaking them down, making them cry, quit, or just lie there, but did he think I was weak? Did he think I was strong and wanted to try me on for size? And this is just the beginning of the story.

One hundred push-ups later and being down long enough to buy a few acres of prime Oklahoma real estate, then holding my weapon away from my body several times until my forearms seared with pain, I was allowed to join my platoon. I barely had the strength to sling my weapon over my shoulder. But I had won. Knowing that gave me great pleasure, so much so I am sure I couldn't feel the pain anymore.

The next evening I was ready to sleep, but I wasn't about to go through all that again. I took the sling off the top of my weapon, wrapped the sling around my left leg twice, and then attached the sling back on to the weapon. I was ready this time. I fell into a deep slumber. I knew it was a deep sleep, because in the morning I awoke to find my M16 *missing* again!

I found DS Jones with my weapon again. He was slightly easier on me physically this time. I only did forty or sixty push-ups with limited ability to speak or recover in a timely fashion. I still held out my weapon away from my body two or three times. He still berated me and threatened that a Russian was still out there in Oklahoma wanting to slit my throat. But he let me walk away, weapon slung over my shoulder, even more proud that day of being able to withstand his onslaught. This wasn't hell—maybe purgatory, but not hell. I could survive. As I started to walk away, he stopped me. He told me in a normal-volume voice that I was the heaviest-sleeping recruit he had ever seen. I snapped back a snappy comment at the top of my voice that they all seemed to love to hear: "DS Jones, Private Rainosek sleeps heavy so he is well rested to kill the enemy, DS Jones."

Skipping ahead a bit, but I later found out at graduation when he was allowed to speak plainly with us that he gained a lot of respect for me that day and the day before. I was willing to let myself become physically injured before I gave in—I would not break. Like most of basic training time, I learned a little about myself and found room to respect myself more as well.

BLANKET PARTIES

After a while we were allowed to make a phone call home, but it only lasted five minutes, and it was every Thursday evening. We stood in line patiently waiting our turn at the bank of pay phones. You could get very homesick, especially in the beginning, at least for those of us who were eighteen and fresh out of our homes. Some were older and calling their wives, and a couple were even thirty or so.

One Wednesday evening DS Jones found one of our guys, a fellow from New Jersey or New York as I recall, standing at a pay phone talking on it. I don't know who he was talking to, but it may as well have been an undertaker or a morgue after what happened to him. DS Jones had his way with him, but it wasn't too harsh. What was harsh was DS Jones removed all our phone privileges for the next day. No one was going to get to call home because of this idiot.

A lot of times, that's the way it was. Sometimes someone screws up and everybody must pay the price. Once, someone couldn't make his bed correctly, and we all had to strip our sheets and carry our mattresses outside and stand in formation with our mattresses at our side and then carry them back into the barracks and make them satisfactorily in the time allotted, which wasn't much time for someone like Gomer or Country. Soon we'd all find ourselves in formation with our stripped mattresses again and again.

This fellow was a white guy who slept upstairs. That night he was given a blanket party by I don't know who—it wasn't me. I had no idea; it wasn't discussed with me, although I found out later that most knew it was going to happen. My radar instincts didn't work this time. For those of you who don't know what a blanket party is, it's where two or four guys take a blanket and throw it over a person's face, abdomen, and arms to hold him down very tight to his bed, and others come up and beat him on the face, chest, and stomach. This poor guy got it bad. He was severely injured. I'm not sure whatever happened to him. He disappeared from our platoon. I assume he had to go to the hospital and lost too much time to join back with us and had to start over. Maybe he broke, quit, or just plain lost it. I don't know. It sure taught most of the rest of us not to try to sneak off and do something we weren't supposed to.

Remember when I said I was going to get back to talking about the segregation in our barracks? Well, here it is. The "brothers," as they were called, a small group of some of the Black guys downstairs, took to liking giving blanket parties to white boys. It all started with the first bunk on the east side. They would come up in the middle of the night, obviously when there was someone on guard duty who didn't mind or was too scared to say anything, and give a mini blanket party to a white guy. I call it "mini" because they wouldn't hit anyone in the face, nor would they leave any marks. As some who got one said, it was a surprise but wasn't as bad as they thought it would be—maybe they would get the air knocked out of them. It didn't happen every night, but when it did it was in a row. You knew when your time was coming up. I was on guard duty one night, and Lando and Latta came sneaking into the barracks. I could tell they had been drinking. I thought about waking up whichever DS was on duty for the night but thought better of it and told them if they would shut up and go to bed, we could all forget this. Yes, I broke the rules—I admit it. But these were my comrades, the guys I was willing to die for and who would die for me.

I awoke the night Gomer, the guy who had the bunk above me, got his mini blanket party. I guess I don't sleep as heavily as DS Jones thought, especially with all the feet shuffling around my bunk, which was noisy stuff. I was next in a night or two. I wasn't too afraid because everyone else lived through it just fine, but I was reluctant to just simply allow it—but how?

I awoke one morning to find that the person sleeping to the south of me had received a blanket party. He was surprised, but I was delighted. The brothers had passed me over. I suppose I had gained my pass the night that Lando and Latta came in drunk. Latta later became a very good friend of mine. His life turned out to be a bit of a tragedy, but deep down he was a good man and became a good soldier.

The mini blanket parties soon came to an end. I think word had gotten to DS Jones, and he had a little talk with those he thought were responsible, and the row was never finished on the other side of the aisle. At the time I couldn't understand why a group of people would do such a thing, but I guess I can understand it now. We had guys who had nothing their whole lives and seen that white folks did, and they hoarded what they had as well. This was their little way of getting some revenge, I suppose. This story may seem like a tragic story of racism and hate, but I think it was more about finally having a little control. But this was in 1983 and involved a lot of people from the south that had experienced the worst of racism their whole lives. Hopefully everyone has learned something from this story and will continue to learn. I learned a lot about the guys who turned out to be my brothers as well.

OBSTACLE COURSE

When a young person joined the army, or at least when I did, I thought I had the physical tools necessary to do whatever was asked of me. Of course I was wrong. On one of our trips to the woods, we went to the obstacle course. If you watch the movies like I did, you think about running over suspended logs, crawling under barbed wire, and climbing walls. Well, you're right, but there is much more that requires the whole team to figure out how to get over, through, on top of, or under an obstacle. I remember one such structure where two guys were holding my arms while I dangled in the air, and they were trying to pull me up to the next level of this structure. I know this is a confidence-builder exercise, but still your confidence is only as strong as the two people who are trying to pull you up. There were a lot of individual exercises, however, and I got thoroughly stuck on one of them.

This obstacle was two telephone poles, both about twenty-five to thirty feet tall. Each one had pegs screwed into the sides to hold onto and put your feet on to climb. At the top was another pole, horizontal to the ground, which connected to each vertical pole. In the middle was a rope with knots in it. So what you have to do is climb up the vertical pole, finagle your way onto the horizontal pole, and come down the rope. Piece of cake, right?

I watched a few of my fellow recruits go through all the obstacles before I went through them. Remember, you don't want to be first or last. Plus, I learned early in life to watch my brothers to see how to do something or how much I could get away with. It was my turn, and I climbed up to the top, no problem. I had been up on roofs, trees, trailers stacked high with hay bales—I was surely not scared of heights. As a matter of fact, the thought of it never crossed my mind. I got to the top and managed to climb up the horizontal pole. I shimmied over to the middle where the rope was, and I made the mistake of looking down. The height may have been twenty-five to thirty feet, but it may as well have been 200 feet. I froze. I didn't like the idea of coming off the top of the pole to grab a rope on the bottom of the pole. I thought death was imminent. DS Jones was on the ground and was telling me in no uncertain terms that I was coming down. I didn't ask for permission to speak, but I let him know in no uncertain terms that I wasn't.

I was in a pickle. No, I was in a real life-and-death situation with no end in sight. I was stuck, and the only way off was by Cobra helicopter either picking me up or shooting me off. Heck, maybe if that Russian DS Jones talked about would have come by, I would have been an easy target.

The last thing I thought would happen happened. DS Jones climbed up the rope and was just under the pole.

In a calm voice, he told me I could do this and to reach down with my right hand and grab the rope, continue to keep my legs wrapped around the pole, and slide downward with my upper body until my left hand could grab the rope…I don't remember all the commands he gave me to help me down, but I followed them. I was shocked by his demeanor and calm voice, because that wasn't usually his way of motivating anyone to do anything. He slid down a little to make room for me to slip my way down to the rope. I did it! He went down the rope, and I was right behind him. My feet touched the ground, and I was ready to do some push-ups and get hollered at, but it didn't happen. DS Jones showed me that day that he had a heart. He wanted me and the rest of the recruits to succeed, and he was going to help any way he could. I'd still be up there if it weren't for him coaching me down.

Later in the day another obstacle came up that made me apprehensive just looking at it. It was two vertical poles with horizontal poles in between them—basically, a ladder with the rungs being farther apart as you go up. At first the horizontal poles were waist high; the next one was chest high, the next was head high, right up until the top horizontal pole, which couldn't even be reached. The task was to climb up each of these rungs and go over the top one and back down again. As I came up to it, guess who was perched up there more than halfway up? DS Jones was up there giving everyone encouragement, or humiliation, whatever was called for, but I have a feeling he was waiting for me. I began my climb, and at first it was easy, but the first one that was over my head was a little harder, and the one after that was even tougher because you had to climb up the vertical pole to get up and grab the horizontal one. It was a struggle, but I made it over the top again about thirty feet up or more. I didn't look down this time, kept my mind on the task, determined to finish on my own. I made it! I climbed over and back down to the top of the obstacle without so much as a word from DS Jones. I didn't know it until later, but he was as proud of that moment as I was. And from that day forward until this very day, I have never feared heights again. I work on roofs that are forty feet high and can stand on the edge with my toes to the line or even farther. I only do this to freak out my fellow employees who fear heights and who will go no nearer than ten feet from the edge.

I know you're thinking, that's a lot of dangerous stuff—doesn't anybody get hurt? Why yes, they do. We were zip-lining before zip-lining was cool, and we did it without being tied on. A guy fell that day about fifteen feet and landed flat on his back. I never saw him again, but after the ambulance arrived, we heard that he probably broke all his ribs and punctured both his lungs. I was in line, and I saw the whole thing.

THE GAS CHAMBER

Here is another part of training that I was warned about beforehand by my informative brother-in-law. He warned me of the dreaded gas chamber. It was a room full of a certain concentration of basically what is riot gas. We practiced and practiced putting on a gas mask and sealing it in less than nine seconds, another piece of cake. It's easy to do when there is no threat of gas in the area. It's more difficult when you can't see because your eyes are burning and watering, all your nasal juices are running out of your nose and mouth, and you're choking and your lungs are on fire. But could it be that bad?

Every day three guys had to go to KP duty at the cafeteria. Kitchen patrol is what KP means. Mostly it meant washing giant pots, pans, and dishes. We took turns at KP, and luckily on the day my platoon went to the gas chamber, I had drawn KP duty. DS Jones said that one day the three of us on KP would go with another unit. Washing giant pots with stuck-on burned potatoes seemed like a joy considering what I was missing. I remember that one of the other guys with me on KP was a nice fellow from Rhode Island.

We got done with our duty and joined back up with our platoon in the bleachers polishing boots and buckles. We heard the horror stories of our buddies' experience that day. Now more than ever we were happy to have missed it, but we still had the threat that we would go someday. A couple weeks went by, and Rhode Island and I thought that surely DS Jones had forgotten that we hadn't gone. That was fine with us. Mentioning this oversight to our buddies, though, proved to be hazardous, because they didn't like the idea that they had to do something so horrendous and that we didn't. Some threatened to remind DS Jones. We threatened back with wondering how many push-ups a person would have to do for attempting to correct a DS's schedule.

Another week or so went by, and I had all but forgotten about the gas chamber, but one Saturday morning, DS Jones told the three of us to go with another platoon in our battalion to the gas chamber. I didn't like the thought of going, but I really didn't like the thought of going without my buddies. Agony is almost bearable when you're not the only one in agony. The term "misery loves company" is a very true statement. I reluctantly got on the bus with my gas mask at my side. When we got there, they separated us into groups of six to eight recruits. We were to march in the door of the chamber with our masks on. My buddies' experience before told me that I would have to take it off and say my name or answer a question to ensure I was breathing after I took my mask off. I was also told to hold my breath for as long as I could before I was forced to take a breath. Should I trust what my buddies told me?

I had no idea who was in my group of six men when we went in. We marched in and did a left face. We were told to take our liners of our steel pots, then put the liner under the steel pot and hold the steel pot under our mouths about chest high. Oh no—this was going to get messy. I was second in line to march in. I didn't want to be first in, but I wanted to be near the front getting out. We were told to pull our masks off and put them in our pouches. Most, I presume, were holding their breath to put them away. Then the Q and A started—questions like "What is your name?" to "What is your social security number?" My lungs burned like fire, my eyes watered, and I never knew I had so much mucus in my head. Spit and nasty snot flowed from my nose and mouth like I had eaten a gallon of slimy okra. I had about as much as I could stand, and finally we were told to do a right face. The door outside was just a few steps away and the door was open. The guy in front of me collapsed to the floor—he just gave out. I stood there wanting him to get up so we could get the order to march. Some DS screamed through his mask that nobody was getting out until the first man got out. Somehow I held my steel pot and put my right arm under his right armpit and stepped forward, dragging him between my legs while he struggled to crawl along. I should have felt bad about dripping snot from my mouth and nose onto the top of his head, hut he had it coming for falling. I got to the door and felt the first rush of fresh air into my lungs. It felt wonderful to breathe again. I dropped the poor guy and rushed to get out of the way of the doorway, where the smell of the gas still was. We coughed, spit, and wiped our eyes for quite a time when we came out. Some took a knee, but I wanted to stay up and walk the air into my lungs quickly, much like a runner after a race.

It was the worst exercise in my little four-year career. It seemed like whatever unit I was in and was issued a mask, it had a hint of the smell of that gas. You could never clean your mask good enough to wash the smell away, and you never forgot the smell of it. It's with me forever.

At my permanent duty station later at Fort Riley, Kansas, we had to go to the gas chamber there twice more. My keen survival instincts made sure that I didn't go in there again. I didn't need the reminder of what it felt like or smelled like. The first time I had a malfunction with my mask. I was working on putting a little rubber liner, similar to a gasket, inside my nose piece. As everyone was getting their mask on, I was backing up to where I was finally behind a truck and out of sight. Nobody ever noticed me missing. When they all came out and were bent over spitting and moaning, I joined them and faked my way through spitting up my lungs. I could smell the faint smell from the door. That was good enough for me. It worked so well the first time I did it again the second time we went.

Now I know what you are thinking. I didn't do my

training, squirmed out, chickened out, and didn't do what was required of me. I look at it a little differently. I thought it was good training to get out of doing it. It's my little Kobayashi Maru. Remember in *Star Trek II: The Wrath of Khan*, when Captain Kirk was the only one who passed the Kobayashi Maru training exercise, and everyone wanted to know how he did it because the exercise was a no-win scenario? He improvised like I did when it came to the gas chamber. Don't get me wrong—I would've gone through it again and again if I were made to, but the powers that be never noticed my cunning escape. That's on them. I think I overdosed the first time when I dragged that kid out the door with me. I think I got a little too much and too long, and it made me very reluctant, so much so that I found a way to skip it. I promise you, if you ever smelled it once, you would never forget. I can also tell you that due to this exercise, I took the training with putting my mask on quickly very seriously. If this stuff that isn't so bad is killing me, what does the really bad stuff do?

WAR GAMES

One of the times we were on bivouac, we went through war games, where your platoon plays laser tag against one another. For whatever reason the vests and guns were not working, so we did it the old-fashioned way, with blanks in our M16s and judges that told you that you were dead. Mostly I suppose that time was all that we had plenty of. I remember being out there in the woods and thinking war games were about digging a foxhole with that little bitty shovel you were issued, then waiting around on someone else to finish theirs. I often wondered why we weren't issued a mini excavator to pull behind a truck. It sure would have saved some time and left plenty of time to write letters home. Finally one day we were in a fight. The goal was to kill the enemy and capture a tent presumably full of our drill sergeants having a good old time. We were tramping through the woods and came to a clearing with high grass, and just beyond that was a dirt road with more trees on the other side—a great place for an ambush. My platoon moved forward in the grass. I thought we were all going to die, so I made my way to the right, several yards from my platoon. I just had a Radar moment thinking something wasn't right. I was farther back than the front line of my platoon, and when they reached the road, all hell broke loose. There was machine gun fire coming from the other side of the road as well as ours. A judge walked out and was proclaiming my guys dead one at a time. I eased up on the road undetected by the judge. He had his back to me just a few yards away. After the shooting was over and the enemy's guard was down, I rushed into the road and dove into the grass on the other side. I waited for the gunfire, but none came. I crawled through the tall grass and made my way into the tree line. I saw the tent and heard talking and laughter as I came closer. I was unsure of whether I wanted to make myself known. I could just go back and be dead like my platoon was after the ambush and play along nicely and be a middle-of-the-platoon player, or I could storm inside the tent with a full clip of blank M16 rounds and blast the enemy away. I decided to open the flap and announced, "Drill sergeants, you are captured, Drill sergeants." Most looked at me as if unimpressed and "who the hell are you?" Then I spotted DS Jones. He asked where I came from, and I told him I survived the ambush by the road and made it to the tent. We walked out and back to the ambush sight, where it was time to regroup anyway. The judge thought I had not stopped after I was told I was dead. I said no, that his back was to me, and I ran over the road. It didn't matter to me or DS Jones what the judge said, I knew I was right, and DS Jones had a small reason to be proud of one of his recruits once again.

HAND GRENADES

Much like the M16 rifle, which everyone had to have proficiency at, you also had to show a proficiency at throwing hand grenades. I loved hand grenades and I could show off with them. I was a country guy who grew up throwing rocks, acorns, corncobs, just about everything you can throw at anything that could be a target. I had great aim if I didn't throw as hard as I could, which made my baseball career short as a pitcher. With proper coaching I could have been OK, but most kids feared standing in the batter's box with me on the mound. I'd rear back and let one fly, harder and faster than anyone in the league, and no telling where it was going. If I slowed it down, I could hit anything, and the batter could too. But having the ability to hit a copperhead snake with a rock came in handy in south Texas.

First off, I will admit that my form for throwing hand grenades was wrong. You were supposed to lob a grenade so you wouldn't hurt your arm while throwing it. While it resembled a ball, it was a bit heavy by ball standard. I had little control when lobbing it, so I threw it like a baseball, just hard enough to get to where it was supposed to go. I was corrected on several occasions but my ability to throw was on display, so DS Jones didn't give me too much flak over it. Of course, we were throwing dummy grenades, so there was no damage from mistakes, but finally we got our opportunity to throw an actual live grenade—pull the pin and let 'er rip. I watched as my fellow maggots stood in a concrete bunker and lobbed their grenades over the wall. DS Jones was in there with them just in case a mistake was made, like dropping it. That never happened, but I can see where his duty was dangerous with a bunch of ignorant eighteen-year-olds.

My fellow maggots all lobbed their grenades over the wall about ten to fifteen yards. They landed in a sandy area that was about ten yards wide and forty yards long. I was surprised how loud the grenade was. Finally it was my turn. I was given my instructions again on how to hold it, pull the pin, and lob it over. I held it correctly, pulled the pin correctly, but I had to do it my way. I reared back and let it fly. It arched through the sky like a Joe Montana pass. It finally landed and blew up. DS Jones was watching the entire flight. I expected to have to grab a piece of real estate, but instead he told me that he had never seen anyone throw one so far. I even overthrew the forty-yard sandy area.

Now onto the grenade course we went. We were back to throwing dummy grenades again, but this time we had forty targets to lob at and be judged and count the destruction laid at our wake. My judge, a DS, didn't say anything about my poor form or lack of a lob, because I was very effective. I would take my grenade and crawl under some barbed wire or some other obstacle, up to a mound of dirt, just to look over and find an enemy machine gun nest staring at me from five to twenty yards away. I took a good fast look, pulled the pin, raised up on my knees, and threw my grenade as hard as necessary, and most times right into the hole of the nest using the poorest but most effective form possible. If there was a copperhead snake in those nests, he didn't stand a chance. One nest, or bunker, or foxhole, or vehicle after another fell to my ability to drop a grenade right into or on top of the target. If I had real grenades, I would have destroyed the course. Total carnage wreaked by this old snake killer. I don't remember the exact words of my judge, but he was impressed and said something to the effect that I had done the best he had ever seen, which to me is amazing, because how many country chunkers have joined the army before me?

OPIE AND THE SIDEWALK

After about four or five weeks of training, we were getting passes on Saturday night to go have a little fun on post. We were not allowed to go off the post most times, but I do remember once when we got to go to Lawton, Oklahoma, the city next to the post. Opie and I went to the mall and bought tobacco pipes and some tobacco. I bought this cherry tobacco, which was not very good, not that any tobacco is good. In the evening, we would sit in the bleachers and smoke our pipes while we shined out boots.

One Saturday we had some things to do early in the day but were looking forward to getting a leave that evening. You really had to try hard not to screw up more than usual, because the threat of missing a leave was always there, and it always seemed to happen to somebody.

There was really nothing to do on leave except go to this little pizza place on post where you could feast on pizza that was like frozen pizza in a grocery store freezer section. They did happen to have ice-cold draft beer. Other places had Mickeys in that little barrel-shaped bottle, and it was fine, but cold draft beer is hard to beat, although I don't remember the brand. Another thing to do was use a phone for more than five minutes. I'd get a pocketful of quarters and call friends at home. When I called my family, I'd always called collect. But with friends there always came that constant interruption of the conversation, "If you want to stay on the line for two more minutes, please deposit seventy-five cents." It was worth it to hear familiar voices.

Another thing we liked to do on leave was go to the activity center, where they had turntables with earphones where you could play records. I never learned to play an instrument or sing worth a lick, but music has always been important to me since I was a child. I'd get records of my favorites from the record library at the activity center. I really liked the Police, the Bangles, Joan Jett, Journey, Boston, and AC/DC, to name a few. I also listened to my outlaw favorites like Waylon and Willie. A new record came out, and it had a song on it by Willie Nelson and Merle Haggard called "Pancho and Lefty." I got that record every time I went there and put on my headphones and listened to it repeatedly. The song mesmerized me, as a lot of Willie songs do.

Anyway, back to the story. My buddy Opie did something to get himself in trouble with DS Jones. While the rest of us were given a pass to go out for the evening on post, Opie had to stay back and pull weeds out of the cracks in the sidewalk in front of our barracks. Opie was devastated. I started to walk away and had thoughts of going to the activity center, but I turned and looked at my buddy, despondent, on his knees pulling out little sprigs of weeds from the cracks. I came back, got on my knees, and started to help with pulling the little weeds. There were hardly any weeds there to speak of, just one little one here and there, about as sparse as my grandma's garden. Opie asked me what I was doing, said that I was going to get both of us in even more trouble. I told him to trust me. I was going to either get him out of this chore or at least help him finish faster so he could go on leave. Soon DS Jones came up and asked me what I was doing. I said, "Drill Sergeant Jones, Private Rainosek is helping Private Opie with this task so he can have time to go on leave, Drill Sergeant." He stood there for a few long seconds, silent. I had plenty of time to wonder if I had done something good or bad. Finally, DS Jones said for both of us to get out of there and go on leave. We thanked him using the usual way to greet drill sergeants as we scrambled to our feet to get the hell out of there before he changed his mind. Opie was incredulous and wanted to know how I knew he would let us go. I told him that I thought he might be touched by a buddy helping a buddy voluntarily. DS Jones was hard, but he was also fair, and he loved to see teamwork. But as time went on, he started to soften ever so slowly, and

I recognized it and tried to use it to my advantage when necessary. Luckily it wasn't necessary very often. I still tried to stay in the shadows of others, the middle of the pack. That was a hard enough feat as it was.

PT TESTS

When we first arrived at basic, we had to do a physical training test. At the time the standard was a minimum of forty push-ups and forty sit-ups in two minutes for each one and running two miles in less than eighteen minutes. Piece of cake for a high stepper like me. My first PT test had me doing push-ups in front of a DS from another platoon. He was tall and had hair from his chest halfway up his neck. He shaved from his jawbone down an inch or two, but the rest was pure hair, like a bear—the strangest thing I had ever seen, and he was downright intimidating. I began my push-ups, and he called them out for me. "One, two, three, three, three—go all the way down to where your upper arms are parallel to the ground. Four, five, six, six, six, six—get down, Private. Seven, eight, nine, nine." I felt like I did about sixty push-ups, but after two minutes, I only mustered twenty-one good ones, according to my hairy judge. I guess I failed that part. Time for sit-ups. I passed with a little more than forty, but my stomach muscles were burning.

Time for the run. Back in school I was fast. I never bothered trying to run any farther than the 440 because my speed didn't help much to win the race. The problem,

I suppose, was I didn't know how to breathe or to pace myself properly. I ran that first two-mile test in barely under eighteen minutes. I came into basic training at five foot ten and 202 pounds—a little pudgy but strong, I thought. DS Jones and DS Ramirez ran us to the ground during those thirteen weeks. We marched even farther, going twenty-four miles one day in a march with our packs on. The longest we ran at a time was a volksmarch, a race of sorts on post. We ran it in formation, as did other units. We came in first on the fourteen-mile run. After we were done with the volksmarch, we waited for the bus to arrive to take us back to our barracks. DS Jones asked if were ready to take off running back to the barracks, about three miles. We were still basking in the glory of winning the race of units in formation, so we said sure. It was a little tough to get back going again after stopping, but we took off singing at the top of our lungs.

DS Jones wouldn't let me, and a few others eat any potatoes and gravy at the mess hall. He was trying to shape us up. Not filling my plate was not a good thing for my fellow recruits, however. At mealtime we stood in line to get our meals. We stood with our noses almost touching the person's head in front of you. "Make your buddy happy" was what that way of standing in line was called. When you got to the front door, one of our drill sergeants was there asking general questions, and if you got the questions wrong, you did some push-ups and went to the back of the line. There was also a chin-up bar right by the door that was put to good use as well. Sometimes you were asked a question that had no good answer. I was asked one time by DS Jones, "Do you have any sugar in your blood?" I thought for a second, wondering which was the right answer. I finally said yes. Man was that a wrong answer. Sugar in your blood signified that you were a gay person, which was frowned upon back then. He gave me a rationing of crap about it, and I did some push-ups. When asked again I changed my mind and said no. Wrong answer again. Now I was threatened to get kicked out because I was unhealthy and unfit for this man's army. I couldn't win.

Another story comes to mind about these loaded questions. DS Jones asked a recruit one time if they were buddies. The recruit said yes. *Wrong answer!* That poor guy had to get down and do quite a few push-ups, twenty at a time, of course, along with the usual repetitive request to speak and recover. After each push-up, this recruit had to say, "DS Jones was my buddy, but he ain't my buddy no more." After a few more push-ups and getting berated, the poor recruit was asked again, "Am I your buddy now?" The recruit said no. *Wrong answer!* Now the recruit had to do more push-ups because DS Jones suddenly felt offended because the recruit did not like him.

In my family there were five of us kids, and I was the youngest, and during mealtimes, if you wanted seconds,

you had better be able to keep with the siblings, especially the brothers that I had. I had to learn to eat fast.
This was both a blessing and a curse in basic training.

Our hard-and-fast rule at first in basic was when the
first guy was finished, everyone was finished whether
they were finished or not. Don't dog it, don't chew too
long, and certainly don't talk during mealtimes. We were
watched, and lots of guys were berated for taking too
long and wound up throwing their chow away. Missing
my potatoes every meal allowed me to breeze through
my meal in no time. Others had barely sat down and
gotten anything to eat and were gulping their trays on
the way to cleaning them. I wasn't very popular with
a few of my fellow recruits at mealtime. Coleman had
mentioned that I should be at the end of the line every
day so I could get my chow last. Good idea, but it didn't
match with my plan of never being last at anything. I did,
however, try to stay toward the back, but if someone
were to get a question wrong, and there were bound
to be a handful, and sent to the back of the line, they
were out of luck. They had better swallow fast when
they got in there, because I was not getting a question
wrong so someone could have spare time to eat.

Running was not the worst exercise we did. We had
this exercise called the fire drill. How it worked was
every recruit ran in place and the DS would give out
a command to do a particular exercise like push-ups,

sit-ups, or any number of other exercises we did. They would also say, "Back," which meant we were to go to the ground and lie on our backs, or "Front," which meant our stomachs. Each was followed by an "up," which meant to get back to our feet and run in place. This exercise proved to be agonizing. A few of my fellow recruits lost it during this exercise; they would go to the front or back and not be able to get back up. Some wanted to scream or fight after a while because they had had enough. A few of them were led away from the field never to be seen again. Opie had a saying, "They won't kill us—otherwise there won't be anyone left to fight." Some days I sure thought they may be trying to kill us with that fire drill. My lungs would start to burn, and my legs would turn to jelly, and I couldn't get enough air but just kept going.

At the end of basic and AIT, it was time to go through another PT test to see how much we had improved. After all those push-ups and miles logged, this was going to be the easiest day of the entire training period. I maxed out the push-ups and sit-ups with eighty each. It was all that was required and what was written down, although I could do a lot more than that in that time frame. We ran our two miles on a track, around eight times. I finished at 12:06. I remember this because I was so unhappy that I was seven seconds off being in the elevens. I came in at 202 pounds, and

I left at 177 and much more in shape than I had ever been in my life.

We started basic with sixty-five recruits, and at the end of AIT, we were down to the low to midthirties. Not everyone got kicked out—some got hurt and had to sit out a while and then start over in another unit. I remember one had a hardship at home of some sort, but the rest couldn't make it one way or the other. Gomer, for instance, did not make it. He was a nice guy, but he couldn't learn to make his bed properly, and having the bunk above me was not good for my bunk being made properly for very long when his got stripped or the whole rack got turned over by an upset DS. I even took to helping him and showing him how to make his bunk, but that didn't help much. He was a little slower at learning things than others, and that was his downfall in the end. Same with Country. We had a few that couldn't cut it physically no matter how many potatoes were withheld from them. One fellow was really large and couldn't do one proper push-up or sit-up. He went through hell for a week or so, but finally he left. I felt sorry for him. He was quiet and never talked to anyone and wouldn't engage if you tried to talk with him. His skin was white as snow, and he had light blond hair. Being in Oklahoma in July was not a good place for him. I thought he was severely homesick, but now I really think he was depressed as well. Homesick guys would cry sooner or later, and I never saw this guy cry.

He didn't last long, two weeks maybe, but he comes to my mind sometimes, and I wonder where he is.

Graduation came, and DS Jones had really lightened up his mood. He had done his duty well. He turned some horrible recruits into soldiers who were ready to fight and die for their country, and we were. Bravo Platoon, the company with the hairy DS, was named best platoon. DS Jones had us in formation, and he gave us that news about Bravo Platoon, and we were downhearted. He told us that sometimes in life you must understand a little thing called politics. You know you're the best, they know you're the best, but because you were also the best the last time, you cannot be named the best this time—you've got to let someone else have the title even though they're really not the best this time. He wasn't too brokenhearted.

My mom came to graduation with my brother-in-law Robert, my sister Wanda, and my two nephews, Aaron and Ryan. We all drove home to south Texas together. It had been only thirteen weeks, but what a journey it had been; I was ready for the next chapter.

A quick word about DS Jones. He was hard, he was tough, and he demanded the most out of you both physically and mentally. He was also one of the men I most respected in my life, and it was a pleasure to know him. Sometime around graduation he told me that he liked me because I didn't know when to quit. Thanks to him, I still don't.

ARRIVING AT FORT RILEY, KANSAS

To say it was a hot summer in Oklahoma that summer of 1983 would be an understatement. Lots of days over 100 degrees, several days over 110 degrees. It would come to be known as one of the hottest summers on record in Oklahoma. We got sprayed with water hoses regularly and had to drink a canteen of water every hour. The winter of 1983 was also one of the coldest winters ever in Kansas. To a poor Texas boy who had never seen snow accumulate on the ground, this was a rude awakening.

I arrived much like I left Fort Sill, gung ho and ready to kill or be killed. I found that regular duty was not what I was accustomed to, although it didn't take long to acclimate myself. It was still military duty, we had a job to do, and we wanted to do it well, but it wasn't drill sergeant run, so to speak. My first platoon sergeant was Sergeant First Class Parker, or "Smoke," as platoon sergeants in the field artillery are known to be called. Smoke was Black, a very tall man—six foot seven or better—pigeon-toed, and he stuttered badly at times. He had scars on his face. Some say he acquired them in Vietnam as a war prisoner, but I never knew for sure.

Our first sergeant Burfict, "Top," as first sergeants are called, was a great man, one of the best I ever knew. I can still hear his voice today. He had a very quiet but commanding voice. Nobody messed with Top. He was a short man, five seven maybe, Black, a rough-and-tough, strongly built 180 pounds. He had forearms like Popeye. Top liked me, and I liked and respected him. He was big into playing organized sports on the post; softball and rugby were his favorites. I didn't care for rugby because I like my teeth too much, but I played it because he wanted me to. Softball was more my game. It's said that high-ranking people demand or deserve respect. I suppose that's true, but guys like Smoke and Top commanded respect. They got it because they earned it—you could just see they were upright guys.

I don't remember my first section chief's name. I found out that he had been a supply sergeant for quite some time before being reassigned to an actual gun crew. I think he had to get some time in on a gun to be promoted to the next rank. He was a nice guy but hardly knew enough about the eight-inch howitzers themselves to be an effective section chief. Our gunner was a character, Sgt. Kenny. He was essentially my tour guide when I arrived. He was a normal-sized fellow, Black, looked like a young Michael Jackson and danced like him too. Sgt. Kenny knew every step to the "Thriller" video. He could moonwalk in his jump boots. He found out I was from Texas, and he insisted that I liked Black jokes and would tell me a joke, one after another. The jokes were terrible, but he was funny telling them. He was only an E-5, but he was what we called "squared away." He was a fine young soldier, and I knew him and his wife for a very long time.

Most of my platoon from basic came to Fort Riley as well. My boy Opie was there and was quickly assigned as the captain's driver. I was assigned to Alpha Battery, five section. Our gun was affectionately known as the Argument. "The Argument" was stenciled on the tube of the howitzer. Legend says the reason it was call the Argument was because it would argue with you as to whether it would run that day. I found it to be true, and I was assigned to the Argument for all my time in the Third Battalion, Sixth Field Artillery Regiment. Alpha Battery also had two other guns, the fourth and sixth sections.

M110A2 HOWITZER

To understand some of the stories you will read in this chapter, it is important that you know how this howitzer works. The M110, which will now be called a gun from here forward, is a self-propelled howitzer, meaning you can drive it like a tank. It has tracks and a big gun tube sticking out the front. The shells for this gun are about twenty-four to thirty inches tall, as memory serves, and weigh 202 pounds. The gunpowder is separate from the shell, and it comes in bags that are numbered five, six, and seven. Depending on several variables, you may shoot a round downrange and use only the bag with five on it. The other two bags go back into the metal canister they all came in. Sometimes you use the six without the seven. It all depends on how far you are shooting the round, the projection of the round, variables as I mentioned. So if a command for a charge five came down the radio, you would only use the five bag, and the six and seven bags would go back in the can. If a charge six was commanded, you put the five and six in but not the seven, and if commanded a seven, you put the five, six, and seven in the tube.

The round comes with a handy lift ring screwed into the top. It comes in handy for loading and unloading. To arm the round, you take the ring off and screw on a fuse. There are two different types of fuses that we used. One was a timer fuse where you had to set it to a particular time that we were given over the radio. The other was point detonating, which means it exploded when it hit the target. The inside of the tube has spiral grooves in it, which causes the round to spin in a spiral when it comes out, like a football. For a point detonation fuse to be armed, it must rotate three times very fast, or at least that's what they told me. On the back of the gun is a spade, a big bulldozer type of blade that you drop down into the ground. When the gun is being put into position, the spade is dropped, the driver backs up, and the section chief operates the spade until it is dug in deep. The reason for this is so the gun doesn't rock backward during recoil. After the gun is dug in, it gets laid, which is something I never got involved in, but it entails the platoon sergeant using a survey type of instrument so he can tell exactly where the gun is located on the map. At this point a little scope-looking thing called a collimator is put in the ground just off to the gun's left side and is pointed up toward the gunner's seat. The gunner aligns his gunner's sight crosshairs with the crosshairs inside the collimator, and with that and the survey sight from the platoon sergeant, the gun is pointed in the right direction, and the good folks at the fire direction center take this information and figure out what is needed to hit a target in the landing zone.

Another track vehicle called an ammo carrier, M548, is parked at a right angle to the blade and the left side, the gunner's side of the rear of the gun. The gun has a cradle that operates hydraulically, and it folds down to the ammo carrier where a round is loaded with a fuse and then locked in and brought back up to the gun, where it can by hydraulically rammed into the tube. The tube must be at a particular elevation for the cradle to line up with it and ram the round correctly. Got all this? Now a guy in the back of the ammo carrier takes the correct amount of gun powder and gives it to the soldier who is going to fire the weapon. He closes the breach, puts a primer in the breach, and latches a lanyard onto the breach and gently pulls—not jerks—the lanyard to fire the gun. Yes, there are lots of variables and rules, and we'll get to those as we get to them. This is the basic idea. A round when exploded can destroy everything within a seventy-five-meter radius of the landing point. If you're within 150 meters of it, you had better be in good cover.

FIRST TIME: BLOWING UP THE WRONG STUFF

I hadn't been off the plane for very long and unpacked my stuff before we went into the field at Fort Riley. I don't ever remember any of my crew members at the time except for Sgt. Kenny, who was our gunner, and another fellow, Griggs, who was our driver. We had a lot of brand-new soldiers like me in the crew and, like I said, a chief who came from supply and hadn't been on a gun crew in a very long time. I had two jobs. One was called the forward advance. As a forward advance, I went to the sight where the guns were going to be coming in later. I put up two long stakes for the gun to park next to so that Smoke could look at the approximate place I needed to place the stakes to be pointed in the right direction. We would also run communication wire from gun to gun and a radio set in the grass. When the guns would arrive, I had to run ahead of my gun and bring it in on the stakes, being careful that nothing ran over the wire. After the gun got dug in and laid, and the ammo carrier got in position, we put up a camouflage net over the two vehicles. Camo netting is a pain in the ass. It wants to cling to everything and snag on every bolt and sharp point on anything. I hated putting on camo netting more than anything.

This trip was in early to mid-November, and it wasn't very cold yet. Typically early in the week was used to practice moving from sight to sight. Getting into position fast and getting laid was a task that needed to be practiced as much as the actual shooting of the gun. Usually on Tuesday a truck came out and delivered ammo to us, around thirty to forty rounds. We didn't get busy shooting it until Wednesday, all into the night and into Thursday. Sometimes we'd shoot very fast and sometimes only once an hour. This time I think was on a Wednesday afternoon, and we were just beginning to shoot the first round. "Fire mission!" came the command on the radio, the one thing every red leg artillery man wants to hear. "Fire for effect" was the next command, which is what you would hear when shooting for the first time in the position you're in. "Fire on my command, PD fuse, charge five, deflection 2116"—which is how to position the tube side to side—"quadrant 316!" (The quadrant command is how to position the tube up and down.) During the command the cradle is lowered to the ammo carrier where a round is loaded, latched in, and brought back up. As soon as the quadrant is given over the radio, the round is rammed into the tube. As this is going on, one of the crew members takes the powder charge that is called and hands it to the person who is to pull the lanyard, which was me this time. I put the powder charge in the tube behind the round and closed the breach. At this time the tube can begin moving up and left and right as needed. I attached a lanyard and waited until we were ready. Finally, over the radio, "*Fire!*" I pulled the lanyard. *Boom*!!! Smoke was everywhere. The sound was deafening, even with ear plugs. Even with the spade dug in, the gun rocks and recoils. It's pretty damn cool shooting a howitzer. After you shoot your first round from site, you leave the tube, and everything sits just like it was when you shot. The forward observers see the round land and make sure they are in range of what the target is. We waited for the all clear to lower our tubes and get them open ready for the next, but it never came. Word got out that only two rounds were seen. The third could have been a dud, meaning a round that didn't explode. Smoke came down to each of the guns to check the deflection and the quadrant to make sure the guns were pointed in the right direction. Everything was fine. He then asked to see the unused six and seven bags of powder. We investigated our used canister to find that it was empty. We had shot the six and seven charge along with the five, about another ten pounds' worth of gunpowder. What a huge mistake. Somehow it was discovered that we had put a giant hole where an M16 shooting range was just seconds before. Thank God the range was empty that day. That could have been the biggest disaster in Fort Riley history if a platoon had been out there shooting. Needless to say, our section chief went back to supply after that. I was partly to blame as well, I suppose. In my excitement of it being the first round that I would shoot in the span of four years, I didn't recognize that a charge seven was handed up to me. The recruit that handed it to me didn't hear, or remember, or just didn't know what he was doing. Something tells me he was a little excited, whoever he was. But an inexperienced crew with an inexperienced crew chief could lead to disaster, and it did. I learned something very important that day. This was not a game; this was real life and real death if something wasn't right. When I finally became a gunner in the next couple of years, I learned to recheck my job and recheck others' jobs as well if there was any question. You can't be too careful. This came into focus on several occasions.

FREEZING TO DEATH

On the next occasion we were in the field it was cold, or colder than I could ever imagine. The three of us that were forward advance went out in a nice warm vehicle called a gamma goat. At night it was Smoke's home away from home and with the heat I could see why. The guns didn't have heat. The ammo carriers did, but an entire section could fit in the cab, plus running vehicles all night was slightly frowned upon, except for Smoke's gamma goat, of course.

We got to the next site, laid out our stakes, and got the commo wire run, and then we all went back to the gamma goat and sat down. It was hot. Here I was in every piece of heavy winter equipment, my parka and fur-lined hat, gloves, everything I needed to do my job until the gun showed up with the rest of my gear, which included a very nice heavy winter sleeping bag.

Let me tell you this heavy winter sleeping bag was worth its weight in gold and silver. The key was to take off your boots and uniform and lie down almost completely undressed. So many people wanted to jump in with their clothes and boots on, and that was a mistake. You would get warm all right—too warm, and then you would sweat your clothes and socks wet and get up the next morning and be even colder and in even worse danger of frostbite. Typically you only brought your one uniform, maybe one more set, but that's it. Oh yes, it's cold nearly naked at first, but the down inside soon warms up with your body heat, and it is pure bliss. I wish I still had mine today.

Anyway, we were in the gamma goat, and we had an AM/FM radio playing inside, and I distinctly remember the announcer saying that it was minus thirteen degrees that night. Luckily, I also noticed there wasn't a bit of wind and about eight to ten inches of snow on the ground. The guns were coming! We piled out of the warm gamma goat to go to the entry and lead our guns and ammo carriers in. First was gun four. On the right bottom of the gun was stenciled what gun it was. We were allowed flashlights to get them identified as well as lead the way for the gun so we wouldn't get run over by a thirty-one-ton behemoth in the dark. The next gun would be mine. I checked, but it was gun six and its ammo carrier as well. Six's forward advance took his gun to their stakes. Where was mine??? Where was my gun and ammo carrier that has all the rest of my gear except for what I was wearing? Where was my warm, toasty sleeping bag? The guns pulled in, but it was decided that laying the guns and putting up the net was going to wait until tomorrow morning. Go to sleep was the order for the rest of the night.

I wandered about and found the gamma goat. I opened the back door and said, "Smoke, my gun didn't show up and—"

He cut me off. "Cll..lll..lll..ose the mother-f#$%^ing door!"

Remember I said Smoke had a stuttering problem. I closed the door and stood outside. I decided to exercise. I did some jumping jacks and found a log to sit on. I was dressed well but still was very cold. I went to gun four, which had a section chief who was Samoan. Let me tell you something about Samoans. I didn't know this section chief or any other Samoans at the time in my life, but I found out quick that you listen to what they have to say. They are fearless; they don't talk shit. If one were to say something that seemed remotely like talking shit, you would soon find out they were not talking shit. Sgt. Fuiva was his name, I believe. He always said when he got a little pissed off that he would choke your mother-f$%^&ing ass! He said it so often that we often made fun of him, not in his presence of course, but I would imitate his voice as best I could and say his famous line. Finally, one day months later, his gunner pissed him off. Sgt. Fuiva grabbed him by the throat with both hands and took him down to the ground. It took a few of us to get him off. He was actually choking his mother-f$%^&ing ass!

I walked to gun four, and everyone was in their sleeping bags in the back of the ammo carrier. I asked, "Do you guys have an extra sleeping bag?"

"Get the f$%k out of here" was the reply I got.

I had been at Fort Riley less than a month, didn't really know anybody except my own crewmates, and they were not here. I was beginning to see the sorry state I was in that night. I took a trip to gun six, where the chief was a Puerto Rican guy. I never worked for him all my time there, but I really liked this guy. He reminded me of the character Mono on the TV show *The High Chaparral*—always smiling, kind of mumbling very low in a Spanish accent while smiling at you. Most of the time, I didn't know what he said, but it sure seemed friendly enough, except for this night when we met under less-than-ideal conditions. Everyone was in their sleeping bags, and I asked if they had an extra. Of course they didn't—everyone brings his own—but it was worth asking. I don't remember the exact words, but it was something like, "Get the f$%^k out of here!" I continued with the sporadic jumping jacks.

Some push-ups against my fallen tree and jumping jacks later, I realized I couldn't go on like this all night. I was cold, and it was getting colder. I realized that this might be it, or at the very least, I was going to get frostbite. I sat there on that log contemplating how desperate my situation was. Perhaps if I went back to Smoke? That big six seven stuttering giant would listen to my plight. Shortly thereafter as I was walking about, I saw a light in the distance like the northern star that the wise men followed. I walked toward the light. It disappeared but would reappear at times. As I got close, I could hear a motor running, which meant heat! I finally came up to it, and it was a vehicle that had a tent attached to the back of it. I fumbled into the tent wall until I found the flap, and I stepped inside. There were guys lying down on cots in their T-shirts in the heated little tented Taj Mahal. Someone said to get the f$%^k out of here, but I was desperate and said in these exact words, "We can all be some fighting mother-f$%^&ers in here, but I ain't going nowhere. My gun and ammo carrier didn't show up, and there is nowhere else to go." They were either too scared to fight or too tired to bother with me, but one finally decided that if I were to watch the radio all night I could stay. *Deal!* Hell yes, I found a place to stay. The radio was in the back of the vehicle where the heat was coming from. It was very hot in there, and I peeled off my clothes, sat in a very tall chair in front of the radio, and promptly fell asleep. Knowing my propensity to stay asleep through everything including DS Jones stealing my M16 twice, I did worry about sleeping through a radio call, but the guns didn't get laid so there were going to be no fire missions tonight, so what the hell. An article fifteen was better than freezing to death. The next morning some of the guys were stirring about, and I awoke to a silent radio. I got dressed and thanked them for saving my life. I found out I spent the night with the fire direction center, the guys who give us the fire mission info.

It was a beautiful clear morning, cold, no wind, but the sun on my face felt like being on the beach. I wandered back over to the guns, which were some distance away. I wandered about watching the crews put up their camo nets, and soon after, a familiar noise of a diesel motor came charging in followed by an ammo carrier. It was the Argument! I ran into a position to wave them down and grab them and lead them into position. As soon as the gun was laid and we were ready to shoot, if necessary, I asked, "Where the hell you guys been? Y'all left me out here to freeze, dammit!" They explained that they broke down and decided to wait until morning to repair it and bedded down on the side of the road. A fuel pedal linkage had come apart, a ten-minute fix, and I was left for dead because of it. I don't remember that crew chief's name then either, but I had a few words for him. He told me something to the effect that he knew I would come up with something. Funny I can remember the guys I liked and respected but can't remember the names of the guys that I didn't respect.

I know what you're thinking—I sometimes think the same thing. Where is all the teamwork, the caring, the willingness to die for each other? I guess all that goes out the window when it's below zero. I could have been more forceful, especially with Smoke, but I was a timid eighteen-year-old with no military rank who didn't know anyone. If I hadn't seen that light, I'm sure that I would have opened that gamma goat and stepped on inside no matter what Smoke said and sat on the floor curled up in my heavy winter parka.

ANOTHER COLD ONE

Later that winter it was some other new recruit's turn to be forward advance. We had a crew full of new recruits, and everyone had to learn all the different duties. The gun had what was called a weatherization kit on it. It was a tarp tent over tent poles that bent over to connect to each other over the middle of the turret. The front of the gun and the tube were still out in the elements. The driver was in the front. There was a hole that the driver had to drop down in. It was right next to the engine, so it was loud in the driver's pit. I don't really remember what job I had traded for, but I was riding under the weatherization kit with our new crew chief, Sgt. Valencia. It was a cold time once again. We were going along, and the gun decided to argue with us—broke down on the side of the road again. Our driver, Griggs, a big, strong, crazy fellow from Missouri, pulled over, and we quickly started searching for the problem. It took a while to fix it, and the rest of the convoy went ahead of us and left us behind. We got the motor fired up and started up again. Griggs was driving in the tracks of the snow of the guns ahead of us, and he noticed that the tracks went up a hundred yards or so and turned left. Griggs, never being one to waste time, decided to cut across the field, cut the corner, except it wasn't a field! Suddenly, the entire front of the gun was under water that quickly came up the turret. Sgt. Valencia and I were climbing poles on the weatherization kit trying to keep our boots from getting wet. Griggs was under water! Man, it had been a bad first year. First I almost froze to death, and now Griggs was going to drown! Somehow the gun came to a stop and began to back up out of the water. Griggs had the wherewithal to continue his driving duties even under freezing water. We came to a stop, and Griggs got out and was soaking wet in the cold air. He didn't want to change clothes. He climbed back in, opened the hatch door to the motor, and let the warm air coming off the heated motor come in. He dropped his seat all the way down, closed his cover, and drove using the mirrored view, the way you would see if you were actually being shot at. When we got to the site, Griggs was almost bone dry from the heat of the motor. I was frozen from riding on the back, so I was slightly jealous. Griggs was a tough old bird, and we were glad that even under ice water he was still able to function enough to back the gun out. This isn't the only story I have on Griggs's toughness, though.

GRIGGS'S HERCULEAN STRENGTH

I don't remember if this was the same trip, but we were almost knee high in the snow on site, broke down again. This time, however, this breakdown wouldn't allow us to shoot, and we were loaded down with about twenty rounds and canisters of powder. We had to distribute the ammo to the other two guns in our unit, but the problem was Smoke was upset about our breaking down and being unable to shoot, so he made us physically carry each 202-pound round and the powder canister to the other guns. There were at least two hundred yards on either side of us. The trouble was that only maybe three of us could carry a round that far in the snow, so it was going to be a long day. The weaker members of our section got to carry the much lighter powder canisters. The proper way to load up and carry a round that big was to sit on the ammo carrier and have two guys pick up the round and place it on your shoulder. You put your hand over the tip side of the round to balance it and then stood up and took off on your journey through the snow.

It took a while to unload, and it was physically tough to make the journey repeatedly. Griggs stood about six foot four and probably weighed about 260, looked kind of sloppy and pudgy, but don't be fooled: he was strong, country strong. He wanted to speed up the process, so he decided to have the guys load a round on both shoulders. Four hundred four pounds on his shoulders as he took off walking through the snow. Well now I'm five foot ten and weighed in at about 180 and considered myself considerably strong as well. I remember being able to pick up a bull hindquarter off a hook and placing it on the butcher table, and it weighed in at 460 pounds when I was a high schooler. I could do this too! I had the guys load me up with 404 pounds of pure deadweight. I stood up somehow and took off walking, but each step was treacherous in the snow, although by now we had a good path leading out from underneath the camo net. Trying to balance one wasn't so bad with two hands, but trying to balance two with only one arm each was almost impossible. The reason I say almost is because Griggs could do it. He made it to the other gun. I made it about ten yards outside the net and found myself face down in the snow, the tips of the rounds sticking in the snow and the blunt ends straight up. I didn't make it far. It wasn't the weight so much as the balance, though altogether the weight was tremendous. I picked one up and rolled it up my arm past my shoulder just to slam it into the side of my head. I took off waking with one round once again. We finally got done, but Griggs did the biggest job of it. He reminded me of some of the guys that helped my dad build barbed-wire fence, leaving me shaking my head and wondering how they did that.

Our unit, the 3rd Battalion 6th Field Artillery Regiment, was being slowly disbanded. The eight-inch guns were going away and not going to be used anymore. The multiple-launch rocket systems had pretty much retired the usefulness of our beloved M110A2. It was a slow death, however. Little by little people were being shipped onto other units and other posts, so much so that instead of having a good eight to eleven men on a section, we slowly dwindled down to only four or five and still would go to the field and shoot live rounds.

COBRA HELICOPTERS

I was always amused by helicopters. I wanted to be a tail gunner when I joined up originally, but my eyesight wouldn't let me go near anything on one, so I had to admire them from a distance. When I first got to Fort Riley, the Cobra helicopter was the baddest thing on the planet but was slowly being phased out and was soon going to be replaced by the Apache helicopter. The Apache was deadlier, faster, and better in every way, but the Cobra looked sleek and badass, like a Chevy Corvette that flies. I loved it. The Apache was more mechanical looking, more like what a war machine should probably look like. Ugly.

One day I was riding along on the ammo carrier. It had a fifty-caliber ring mount above the canvas cab of the carrier. I was riding fifty cal one day when going from one site to another. Now vehicles in our unit drove down tank trails a hundred yards apart, and it could be very dusty when dry. If it was wet and muddy, then riding through the hole of an ammo carrier was a great duty if the temperature was comfortable. I was enjoying the ride and singing songs at the top of my lungs because no one could hear me. I was supposed to be paying attention to the surroundings around me so no commies could jump up and get me, but I was lollygagging. I was happy for some reason. I'm sure I was swaying to and fro thinking no one could see me well from a hundred yards away. I was singing the chorus of "True Colors" by Cyndi Lauper. It was a popular song then, and I didn't know the rest of the words just yet. I had a funny feeling that I was being watched. I looked around and finally turned around and there, right behind me, was a Cobra helicopter just hovering, watching me. Another cool thing about the Cobra is that it flew with its nose down. I quickly unlocked the fifty cal on the ring and swung it around to point it at him. I'm sure the pilot got a good laugh out of me since, if he wanted to destroy me, he could've twenty times already—and everybody else in the convoy for that matter, and I was just now spinning around to blast him. He wasn't hovering much higher than we were, but he decided to go play some hide-and-seek games elsewhere. The pilot put the hammer down and flew over the top of me. I didn't ever hear him over the noise of the ammo carrier until he got in front of me. Man, those things were badass!

Another day early in my time at Fort Riley was spent in the field on KP duty. I was washing pots and pans and wasn't paying attention to anything. I was away from the truck that the cooks did their cooking in. I soon had that feeling and heard a hum behind me. I guess the pilot was thinking about having a bit of breakfast. I would have cooked him some myself for a trade to be able to ride along with him one time. Once again the pilot put the hammer down and blasted us with the thunder of the motor. Those things were so cool. Did I mention that before?

SALUTES

In the spring and summer of 1984, my unit drew the assignment of shooting salutes at town festivals and military funerals in the area. A select few of us strapping young men were chosen. All were within five ten and six feet and strong young men. There are many forms of salute, and we used all forms of guns for our twenty-one-gun salutes. For most funerals we used M16s. For town festivals we used towed howitzers. Of course we shot blanks, but even they were cool in that, if we shot at night, the round we used had a form of paper, a lot like toilet paper that came out of the tubes in flames and sparks. First though came the work and practice. It took seven men to shoot a salute with rifles and fourteen to shoot the howitzers. I was on both salute teams, and then came the work and the practice. We would go down to the motor pool and practice every evening. We would stand at attention with our M16s by our sides. The command, "Ready," came, and everyone in unison would lift his rifle up to the ready position. I won't go into every detail about raising the rifle up to that position, but there were steps involved in the movement, and we had to learn to do so in unison. Every step was in unison through the entire process. "Aim" came next, and we raised the rifle up to aim in the air in the same direction and once again in unison. "Fire," again in unison. We had a saying about this, which was "no popcorn," which meant we learned to time the shot together to get one bang, not several bangs. This all took a lot of practice to get the timing down for everyone, and we also practiced marching. After all this time, you'd think we knew how to march already, but doing it in front of an audience, every step, every movement needs to be perfect and automatic and in unison. There was no time to think about it all, just automatic.

The seven of us learned to be perfect, if I say so myself. Our squad leader, Lt. Bacak, a Czech descendant like me and from San Antonio, drilled us relentlessly. I grew to like and respect Lt. Bacak ("LT") not only for our similarities in our backgrounds but because of his ability to lead and teach and his expectation of perfection in himself and us. But I must say that we became friends outside of our military duties due to our being "home boys." He was a great guy.

Next came the howitzers. This took seven guns and two men per gun. We had extra guys join us for this salute. One would pull the lanyard, then open the breach, and the spent casing would eject, and the other man wound catch it coming out and set it down on the ground and shove the next round in, and the first guy would close the breach and be ready to fire again. With rifles the seven of us would shoot together three times to make twenty-one shots, whereas the howitzers were shot one a time. One gun, one shot, one after another, and then come back around to the first gun, which would shoot again for a total of three shots each. We didn't pull out the howitzers but maybe four or five times that summer, but we shot the rifles quite often at funerals. I attended a lot of funerals in those days.

Although I didn't know the person who died, it was always sad. These funerals were for military guys, people who spent their entire career in service of their country.

We shot the cannons at Memorial Day services at Ft. Riley cemetery and July Fourth celebrations at El Dorado Lake, and then we packed up and went to another festival somewhere and shot again. Of course we were dressed to impress. Dress As, shined up jump boots with white laces, pants tied up above our boots to show off our boots, stainless steel pots on our heads— we looked very sharp.

The most fun we had, though, happened in Wichita, Kansas, at their river festival. We were to leave early on Saturday and stay overnight at the local air force base and come back on Sunday. As we were ready to leave, LT was driving a military car, and the rest of us were going to ride a military bus. LT's wife was riding with him, but he wanted to bring his own vehicle so he and his wife could do some sightseeing in Wichita during the day on Saturday. He couldn't use the military vehicle for such activities, so he had to bring his own. He asked me if I would drive it down there for him. Why hell yes, I'd drive his car and skip being on the bus. Air conditioning, radio, and my buddy Latta, who I had let slide coming in drunk in basic and he convinced his partners to pass me up on the blanket party list.

We got to Wichita and took part in the festivities in the daytime that go along with Riverfest, but as evening fell we got serious. Here was the plan. The guns were located on the Douglas Street bridge pointed over the river to the south. The Wichita symphony was in a local building somewhere playing a few tunes. Their performance was being blasted outside by speaker spaced everywhere. I thought it was going to be a sound disaster due to the vast size of the area, but what do I know? They got to the last song, *The 1812 Overture*. Before they started we were off to the side of the bridge and marched on in front of thousands of people on the banks of the river, on the street, everywhere. The bridge, however, was empty except for us standing at parade rest with our trusty howitzers.

Now here is what was going down. *The 1812 Overture*, when played in its entirety, goes for about fifteen minutes. Standing at parade rest if feels more like 1,812 minutes. But toward the end of the song is the part, dona dona dona dont da da, then a boom from a big bass drum. Our job that day was for each gun to be the bass during that song. It's hard to explain so go look it up on YouTube and you'll see what I'm talking about. Also, we had more rounds than what we needed for the song. After the song was over and we were done being in the band, LT gave us the command to *fire at will*!!! I think each gun had at least nine or ten extra rounds, and we loaded and fired them as fast as we could that night over the river in the dark. I loaded and unloaded shells as fast as I could, but I do remember sneaking a peek to my left to see all the paper spewing fire over the water. Seven guns firing fast as they could in a race to see who could fire all their rounds the fastest. I don't remember who won the race, but it didn't matter. It was impressive. Approximately seventy rounds, *boom*, ...*boomboom*...*boom*...going off like crazy. It was fun, probably the most fun I had up to that point in my military career. After a barrage of shells, it was pure chaos. The screaming and applause were thunderous and confusing. LT was screaming commands at us to get back in formation and to march off the bridge again, leaving our guns and spent casings lying about. We got to the barrier of the bridge where all the people were, and we were mugged, but in a good way—lots of people grabbing our hands to shake them, slaps on the back and screaming in our ears, giving us all their gratitude and thanks for the show. It was a very proud moment for me and my gun mates. Suddenly the long hours in the evening into the night were worth it. We celebrated that night. We were in our borrowed barracks, but LT had made sure we had plenty of beer to drink that night. We partook freely, happy to have been a part of such a celebration of Americana.

The next morning we were waiting to load up and go back. I was chewing my Copenhagen like usual and spitting into a beer can. LT came in obviously to give me the keys to his car, but he thought I was drinking my breakfast instead. At the time I had no idea. He walked out. I thought about it and realized he thought the beer can I was holding had beer in it instead of tobacco juice. I chased him down to explain, and he was happy. He was going to tell his wife that she had to drive instead of riding with him back to Fort Riley. Plenty of guys were drinking their breakfast and loaded up on the bus with the extra beer that was left. Latta (my shotgun rider) and I took our place behind the bus going down the highway. Our stupid gun mates riding in the bus were still drinking all the way back. You know what happens when you drink beer—you must go to the bathroom more often. These idiots were urinating into their empty beer cans and then pouring them out the windows of the bus. Here I was cruising along in the AC and blasting the radio when (I don't mean to gross you out but) *whoosh*, a mist of fluid covered the car and windshield. I know urine is waste, and I'm not sure of its true composition, but in this form, it is very sticky and a mess and does not come off easily with windshield wiper fluid. I quickly learned to stay back away from the bus. We got back, and I stopped in Ogden where Mike lived and dropped him off and then quickly went to a car wash and washed off all that sticky urine that was on LT's car. He never knew the difference.

Rifle salutes were different. Funerals were a somber event, even for me. Sometimes we took part in folding the flag, sometimes as a pallbearer, but always shooting the salute—and perfectly, I will add. Popcorn was not wanted at a funeral salute. We traveled by bus, and we had an extra rider. I'm not sure where this guy was from, but he was the bugle player, and he played "Taps." He was kind of a nerd in real life, but he could bring tears to your eyes playing that song. He brought tears to my eyes plenty of times. When I hear it these days, I always think of that nerd at the twenty-one-gun salutes. It still can bring a tear to my eyes today.

I often joke with family and friends these days that I have been to too many funerals in my lifetime. I used to get pulled out of school to be an altar server at funerals during the week when I was a kid, and now in the army I shot numerous funeral salutes as well as served as pallbearer or whatever the family wanted us to do. I tell them that when they die, if they see me at their funeral consider themselves important to me, because I quit going to funerals except for them. Hell, I won't even be at my own funeral.

MIXING IN WITH THE NATIVES

Unlike today where virtually all the population has mad respect for military folks and vets, back then it wasn't always that way. We were always told not to go to town alone. Junction City, the nearest town to Fort Riley, was a true military town. If it weren't for Fort Riley, I don't think it would have been there. It was full of bars, strip clubs, and used car lots. I ventured out by myself in the daylight. Junction City did have a nice downtown area with lots of shops to window shop in. I especially liked a bookstore called the Town Crier. It was chock full of books and magazines. I could wander around this store for hours, read everything I wanted and never buy anything. We liked to go eat at Big Cheese pizza and then go over to Ma's Lounge for beer. It was pure military inside that place, though, no singles at all, so even finding someone to dance with was hard to do at Ma's Lounge.

My friends and I soon started to make our way to Manhattan, Kansas, home of Kansas State University. This, my friends, was what we called a target-rich environment. The male population of KSU didn't like us and we were easily recognizable by our haircuts. I never really saw or felt any danger, but we knew we weren't welcome in the local bar scene close to campus. We frequented a place out on highway 24 called the Ranch Saloon, which was a few miles out of town. It was a country bar with plenty of single people to dance with and get to know. I liked the place, and the more I came, the more the management, bartenders, and bouncers got to know my friends and me and made us feel welcome. It was a considerable distance farther than Junction City, but those Kansas gals made the miles in the trip worth it.

MEETING THE LOVE OF MY LIFE

Being from Texas, I enjoyed music and dancing more than most guys. I like a good band, and the Ranch had bands play there such as the Smoky River Boys and Boogie Grass Fever, which was my personal favorite. They had an original song called "Wild Turkey Whiskey." I still remember the chorus, "Wild turkeyyyyyy, whiskeyyyyyyy, makes me feel all right, had some again last night, I'm smilingggggg, this morningggggggg, thinking about tonightttt…"

I was at the Ranch and sitting at a table with some friends, drinking and having a good time. Along the side of the wall was a raised-up area, only a step up, however, with tables for four along the wall. Each table had a light hanging above the middle of it. I scanned the place and noticed a gal sitting at one of the raised tables with two other gals. She was wearing jeans with a sweater that was dark with thick multicolored horizontal stripes that showed her shape to its advantage. She had blond hair and beautiful eyes, and I knew I'd be reaching, far reaching with a gal like this. I stared for a while admiring her beauty. She was beautiful and one of those you could take home to Mama.

I was oblivious to the conversation around me at the table. I finally said to no one in particular that there was the most beautiful girl I had ever seen, and I was going to ask her to dance with me. They mumbled, "Go ahead," but I made up some kind of excuse like, "This song is almost over; I'd better wait for a new one." The conversation went on at the table, but I wasn't paying attention. Some time passed, and I said again that I was going to ask that good-looking gal over there to dance. They basically said, "Quit talking about it already and do it." I used an excuse—"This song isn't very good; I'll wait for a good one."

I knew I had better hurry; time was growing short. I noticed she got up to go to the bathroom, and she had to go to the other side of the saloon to where the bathrooms were located. She walked right by me, and I watched her go the whole way.

"Damn, I'm going to ask her to dance." I'm sure my friends were rolling their eyes at me by now.

"Better make a move or somebody else will," they said.

She came out of the bathroom and was making her way back. I watched as she got closer and was hoping to get a smile and a look from her. She walked right past my chair without so much as a glance, but she kicked my chair leg. She tripped a little, not enough to fall, and kept on walking. I thought, "Now or never. This is a sign from God. This is my time." I let her sit down, and I came over and asked her to dance. I don't remember her saying no, but I do remember that she said she couldn't dance. It didn't matter what she said, I wasn't taking no for an answer easy. I told her it doesn't matter, but she still refrained. I told her in one song that I could teach her to do the Texas two-step. I don't think she believed me, but she finally gave in and came out on the dance floor with me. That first dance was a short dance lesson. She was a quick study, and she saw immediately how much fun dancing was. We swung around that dance floor several times that night. I was smitten, already in love. I sat with her and her friends, one of whom is now our sister-in-law Brenda. We showed each other our driver's licenses to show off our equally hard names to pronounce. Pam and I talked about our siblings and were amazed that we were both the youngest of five, and the gender order of our siblings was the same with almost the same ages. There are many amazing similarities to our families, and I'm not sure which ones we found out that night, but there were quite a few. At the end of the night, she walked with me to my car, and we kissed for quite a long time. Brenda came close by and announced that she was ready to go and she had better come. I offered to give her a ride but knew she wouldn't take it, nor would Brenda allow it. I got her phone number, and it's been history ever since. That was one of the best nights of my life, certainly a life changer, and I'll remember it forever.

One day early in our relationship, I was doing my laundry. I think she called me and told me that she was going out to the Ranch Saloon that night, a weeknight of all things. I told her I was doing my laundry and couldn't make it. After hanging up I was able to manage to do my laundry so fast that I changed the laws of physics as they pertained to doing laundry. I was so fast, in fact, that I got out to the Ranch, a good twenty to twenty-five miles away, before she did. There I was standing with a pool cue in my hand with my beige cowboy hat on when she walked in. We danced the night away again.

Pam attended K State and worked part-time at a Dairy Queen. I suddenly became a big fan of DQ dipped cones. Pam would make me one, and I'd stand at the counter to talk with her while she worked. I couldn't talk long, and I didn't want her to get in trouble, but I couldn't help it. We continued to go dancing on weekends and spend as much time as we could on the phone on weekdays. Of course, there were no cell phones back then and the barracks had one phone for the entire barracks, so it always seemed it was in use or someone was in line to use it to call in a pizza delivery or something. We always wrote letters back and forth too. (Now there is an art form that has disappeared.) I'd write lyrics of songs of love, some serious, some not so serious. I'd use the lyrics of Merle Haggard, all the way to David Allan Coe and the Geezinslaw brothers. A wide range and no, I didn't use *those* songs of David Allan Coe.

At this point in my time in the military, my priorities changed on a dime. It used to be putting "steel on the hill," a term for putting howitzer shells downrange, but now it was "what time do you want to eat?" My life was changing and for the better. My real-life decisions didn't just include me anymore.

STILL HAVING FUN

Even though I had a serious girlfriend now, having fun with friends didn't have to stop there. My two best friends in the army, Opie and Tom, and I had lots of fun. Some time went by for us. Pam had a roommate, Angie, that eventually became Tom's girlfriend. One Saturday Tom and I decided to rent a V-bottom boat with a ten-horsepower or so motor on it from the rec center on Fort Riley. The four of us went to Tuttle Creek and motored around in that little boat—Pam, Angie, Tom, and me, with a case of Falstaff beer, on sale for $8 a case or something ridiculous like that. Money was short, so sales were important, but I was given a fair amount of crap for buying Falstaff. We decided to get a little more adventurous and drop the boat into the Kansas river in Manhattan and ride it to Wamego, Angie's hometown about fourteen miles away. The trip began fine, but the Kansas river that day was more like a Kansas creek. It wasn't very deep at all, and with all our weight, it was causing a lot of grounding for the prop in some sand banks. We made it about half the way when the motor overheated and wouldn't start back up again. We were on foot. We walked through a cornfield in the dark and got to a road, a little paved country road between highway 24 and the river. We started to hike back toward Manhattan in the dark. A car was coming down the road. It was some kind of sports car. It drove past, slammed on the brakes, and wheeled around like a professional driver. It came back, this time angled toward us like it was trying to run us over. We went into the ditch thinking, "Is this guy serious?" He turned again. Tom and I loaded our hands with pea gravel on the side of the road. As he drove past rather close, we peppered the car with pea gravel. It kept going this time. I was extremely worried that he would come back with friends. We kept walking down the road, and a pickup came driving by, slammed on the brakes, and swung around like a Duke boy. Was this an episode of *The Twilight Zone*? We loaded for bear with pea gravel again, but the pickup pulled up and slowed to a stop. A slow-drawl, familiar voice asked, "Do y'all need a ride?" *Opie*!!! Opie, a little intoxicated, was driving down the road looking for nothing in particular and gave us a ride back to the girls' apartment. We were very fortunate to be found by Opie.

The next morning Pam took us down that little country road. She dropped us off at a cornfield, and Tom and I walked through the cornfield down to the river. We were close to where we tied off the boat, and we started to make our way back to the boat dock. We had better success because there were only two of us in the boat, and I sat on the V and watched for where the current was, which was the deepest part of the river. We made it back in no time this way. It was truly fun now, and Tom tried to throw me several times. We took the boat back, never to rent another again.

TUTTLE CREEK

Pam and I liked to go to Tuttle Creek to walk the creek, hang out on the rocks of the lake on the other side of the dam, even try to fish a little, skip rocks, all kinds of cheap entertainment. We were out there sitting on the tailgate of my pickup, and we were talking about the future, and I kind of proposed to her sitting on that tailgate. It wasn't a one-knee kind of thing, not my most romantic day—really awkward as I recall—but truly a country boy way of proposing marriage. She accepted, but a trip to Germany loomed ahead.

REFORGER

We set a date of May 24, 1986, as our date to be married. In February and March, I had a trip to Germany scheduled, REFORGER is what it was called. It stands for return of forces to Germany, a forty-five-day military exercise than spanned virtually the entire countryside of what was then West Germany. Due to the snow and icy conditions, though, we parked our howitzers—war reserve howitzers, much newer and better than our Fort Riley guns—in a little village. The locals didn't like us much, hid their wives and daughters from us. They really came to hate us when our heater fuel leaked out in the snow and ran down to the fishing pond. We left and came to a military post called Grafenwoehr. We holed up in a barracks there for what seemed like a couple weeks of doing absolutely nothing. They had a beer tent there and a rec center. Every day at the rec center, the movie *Porky's* played daily, over and over. I have never watched that movie again since then. But the beer tent was different. The tent was huge and round with tables around the walls, and an open area—a dance floor I suppose—was in the middle. They only had two servers, so when a table full of people had the waitress come up, they would order a lot of little plastic cups, eight-to-ten-ounce cups. You could have six guys sitting around a table, drunker than hell with up to thirty cups of beer sitting on the edge of the table. I was broke and thirsty, not a dime in my pocket, but I drank plenty of beer. I'd walk up to a table, talk to the guys there like I knew them, slap them on the back and joke and laugh and during the conversation lift one of their many beers while they weren't paying attention. Yes, that was stealing, but they really didn't need it. They had plenty. We left there and went to put away our equipment in Amsterdam. We stayed in the basement of a hotel, sleeping on cots on indoor tennis courts. Nothing happened here except lots of cleaning, volleyball in the gym, and waiting to go home.

C130 AND A BISCUIT

In some place in West Germany, we boarded a C130 military aircraft. A C130 has seats that are metal framed and straps that line the side and middle of the length of the plane. It had cargo netting above our heads to put our gear. We were crammed in there so tightly that some people climbed up to the cargo netting to lie down on duffle bags, thankfully, to give the rest of us some room. It was so noisy as well you could barely talk. After many hours a Styrofoam plate with a biscuit started to make its way down. We handed them down toward the back of the plane one at a time. I was very hungry—we all were—and those biscuits looked pretty good. I was only a soldier or two away from getting to enjoy my biscuit when suddenly, the oxygen masks came down. I'm no expert in flight, but I can say it felt like we fell out of the sky. Very scary with no windows. We landed in Portugal for repairs. We got off the plane and sat in a roller-skating rink. About four hours later, we boarded again, and I never got my biscuit. It was a happy homecoming, however, and now our wedding was right around the corner.

WEDDING WEEKEND

Our weekend was a whirlwind. My family came up from Texas and holed up in a hotel in Harper, Kansas. We had a wedding rehearsal dinner at the Copper Club, and along with my groomsmen, Opie and Tom, I went across the road to the Copper Lounge and had many beers and pool games. I woke up the next morning and played in the park with my nephews. It was time to head to Zenda, and my two groomsmen were riding in one car while I drove Pam's car. I thought I was taking a bit of a shortcut, the shortest route to Zenda, but I didn't know the area as well as I thought. I got a little lost but felt if I kept heading northward, I would run into something I would know. I finally drove into downtown Spivey, a town no bigger than Zenda, seven miles east of where I was supposed to be already. I finally made it to Zenda.

I wore a tuxedo that was white—a big mistake as I quickly became known as Boss Hogg, a character from the TV show *Dukes of Hazzard*. I was still feeling the effects of the beer from the night before, but, standing at the altar seeing Pam for the first time in her wedding dress, I felt instantly better. It was a beautiful ceremony.

My family always gambled at almost everything. My dad and male family members went out into the dirt street and started throwing quarters at a line drawn in the dirt. Pam's uncles saw that something was going on, and they came up and joined in. Pam has a lot of uncles, and there was quite a line of well-dressed gentlemen out in the dirt road throwing quarters. I'm not sure who the big winner was, but I had about ten to twelve dollars in quarters and quite a few dollar bills after it was all done. Over the years every time I would see those uncles at some kind of family function, they reminded me of the time they got robbed by those Texas quarter-throwing sharks.

We had a wonderful fried chicken meal and the local band, the Shifters, Martina McBride's dad's band, played our wedding dance. They had a gal sing a few songs; I'd like to think it was Martina, but I can't verify it, but she is younger than we are so who knows? That day was the start of a very long and wonderful marriage.

HONORABLY DISCHARGED

I had less than a year to the end of my four years of active duty. My best buddies were leaving or already gone. I had received my orders to move from my unit that was being disbanded. I moved down the street to an M109 unit. An M109 was a howitzer that was about half the size of an M110 but could shoot faster. A few of us from my original unit went over there, but it was getting to know a whole new group of people, and now I was married and didn't care about military service anymore except to do what I was supposed to do and that's about it. I wanted to be married to my gal, not to the army anymore. Reenlistment wasn't an option. I had to think about being discharged and what I was going to do now, rather what where we going to do now. I had a very good offer from another army buddy who got out a year earlier who had also gotten married to a local gal.

He wound up staying and working road construction, being an equipment operator. He said he could guarantee a job for me. It paid pretty good money, but I thought I wanted something different. Funny, back in high school, I wanted to leave the classroom and be outside. Now after being outdoors for the better part of four years, sleeping out in it, I wanted back into the classroom. It was time to go to school and learn something and be somebody who knew more than how to make sausage and to kill people.

CIVILIAN LIFE

GOING TO WORK

My time in the army was ending, and I never got to shoot that Russian who was trying to slit my throat that Drill Sergeant Jones was always warning me about. I didn't know what I wanted to do with myself for sure, although Pam and I had choices. I decided to enroll in the DeVry Institute of Technology and attend its campus in Irving, Texas. DeVry had campuses everywhere, but since my folks were in south Texas and her folks were in south Kansas, we thought that being in between the two would make it easier for us to visit either, about a five- or six-hour drive either way. Now I know DeVry has taken a bad rap in recent years, but back then it was a legitimate school. I took the electronics repair program. The only problem was I knew absolutely nothing about electronics except how to turn on a TV or a radio. But the technology aspect fascinated me. I remember as a kid the TV repairman coming out to replace the tube in our old TV, and I thought, how hard is that? My little Texas Longhorn helmet radio that sat on top of a fence posts would get inadvertently dropped by small hands, and the little plastic clips that kept it all together would break and the guts would fall out, but I'd soon have it all back together and tape covering the top of the helmet from front to back. I was a junior repairman already.

I had a check for the GI Bill coming in every month, which took care of the rent and some of the groceries, $525 I think it was. Pam took two jobs, but their hours clashed, and she stuck with one, at Walmart stocking health and beauty aids, and quickly made her way up to the department manager of health and beauty aids. I guess here is good a spot to say this. Pam is a beautiful girl, smart, and can outwork 99 percent of the people at any job she's had. If I had to do it all over again, I would have gone to work at Walmart, and she would have gone to school to learn something to make a crap ton of money at, because she works like a Tasmanian devil when she enjoys her job. Sometimes I feel like she feels she missed some things because I went to school and she never finished hers.

Graduation was coming, it was time to find a job. DeVry had a long list of employers lined up to interview us and all we had to do was sign up. The first one on the line was a company called Recognition Equipment Incorporated. The entire class signed up for the interview. I thought it would be a good opportunity to interview for the very first time in my life, even though there were really talented students who got better grades than me that I thought would probably get the job. I was ready—I had my Men's Wearhouse suit on. I interviewed with a very well-groomed man named Glenn. I thought the interview went well, and it came time to chitchat about hobbies. I told him my main hobby was playing softball. I played on the DeVry team, I played all through the military, and even made this all-artillery team. Glenn was impressed and told me that the company had a softball league that I could play in. I said, "Sure, I'd love to." I was almost hired on the spot. Now just think for a moment. I, middle-of-the-class student out of a graduating class, went to what was supposed to be a practice interview while a valedictorian was supposed to get the job but didn't because he or she didn't play softball and I did. I was either lucky, or Glenn was an idiot. Not to jump ahead, but it turns out both were true.

I wore my cap and gown on a Saturday and went to work on that Monday. I worked in the product repair center, and I was—and I hate to say it—more than just slightly overwhelmed. I learned the basics of electronics from the book. I had no real working knowledge of how a hard drive worked or needed to be erased and formatted again for use in our systems that I knew absolutely nothing about. I worked with a girl named Lynn. She hated me, but then again she hated everybody. She eventually warmed up to me and thank goodness for that—she was unbearable when she was perpetually pissed. My other coworkers couldn't believe that she finally appeared to actually like somebody that wasn't in the office and above her pay grade. We had Kevin Logan, Dennis, a.k.a. Slipfoot Wilson, his blues-harmonica-playing alter ego. We had Donna, who ran the warehouses and answered the only phone in the shop. It was funny because Kevin would get a phone call from his wife about once an hour. We'd hear Donna holler over the whole shop, "*Kevin Loooogan*!!!" She really hung out the Os. I don't know who is responsible, maybe me, but after a while when Donna would yell out his name, the rest of us would holler in response, "Kevin Low," which soon turned into "Kevin blows," which soon turned into "Kevin blows; he needed the money." Kevin was a brilliant technician and should have been an engineer, which he later became. It was long ago, so I don't remember all the names or have stories about everyone, but remember, we have a softball league, and it's coming up.

WANNABEES

Glen told me there was a softball league, but he never said he wanted me to be on his team. His team was made up of all the management and office types of people, not the people wearing lab coats or working in the warehouses. I worked in a satellite building about five miles away from the main Recognition campus. It was a rented building. The league was starting, and teams needed to be formed. Since I wasn't welcomed on to the management team, and others from my department and the warehouse folks weren't either, I looked to form my own team from the people left in the building. It was only a company softball league—it wasn't the big leagues—but still I was too competitive not to try to get a team that could compete. I got a team together, just enough, and if you needed to borrow a player from another team on game night, you could do so—he wouldn't have to be very deep in our rosters. It was coed but only required two women on the team since the company was men heavy. We had to come up with a name, and we were a little sore that the management team didn't want us to play for them, so we named our team the Wannabees, because we all wanted to be on the other team. We had yellow T-shirts with blue letters, *Wannabees*.

The games started, and really, we weren't too bad, for this league anyway, and the management team was rather good. They had about four guys who could play the game well. My team had two: a warehouse guy who was older, had terrible knees, and couldn't run, but he could hammer the ball over the fence most of the time, so he didn't have to run, and me. I talked long and hard to get him to play for us. I camped him out on first base, so he didn't have to move much. Yes, I was the coach, and just talking to him I knew that dude could play, and he could.

A funny but painful story. We had a girl on the team that I talked into playing. She had never played before, but I thought she could learn; after all, I needed bodies to stand in the field. She worked in the office at work, but the management team didn't have her on their team, so I talked her into playing for us. She was a quiet person by nature. She showed up that first day. We had three girls on the team—the other two were Diane and Diane. I put this girl out in right field. That first game she took her position, and sure enough someone hit a high fly ball in her direction. She moved around, put her glove in the air, the ball came down, and splat! The ball went right past her glove and hit her squarely in the left breast! She picked up the ball and tossed it about forty feet in the direction of second base. She proceeded to walk off the field, through the dugout, and straight to her car and drove off without a word. She told me the next day she retired from the game of softball last night. I felt bad for her because, *damn*! That had to hurt, but it was funny at the same time.

The time came for us to play the management team. That team was coached by a guy who had a beard, and I had a mustache. We bet facial hair on the game, loser shave all! Up to this time they were unbeaten, and we were five hundred or so. I was proud of my mustache that I had had since high school and wasn't ready to lose it now. I had a game plan. Our pitcher and I swapped positions. He took the shortstop spot, an important position in this league, since half the players couldn't hit it out of the infield anyway. But against this team, a pitcher needed to have a plan. We played by Amateur Softball Association rules where you're only allowed one foul and after that you're out. They had several players that liked to pull the ball down the left-field line. Our first baseman, the guy with the bad knees, got put over on third base for this one game. We needed a guy who could catch everything there that day, and if he could rise to the occasion just one more time, we might have a chance. The game began. The whole company was at this one because of the funny wannabe story and because of the bet. Every batter started with a one-one count to help speed the game up. Our umpire, who made $15 a game, had a big strike zone because most teams couldn't pitch worth a crap. I pitched one way inside, and the batter would swing and pull it foul. Okay, one ball and two strikes with no fouls left. I pitched one way outside for a ball just to let them know that they have choices. The count was two and two now. Now I scouted this team heavily. Actually I couldn't help but see them play since every team played on Tuesday and we sat around and drank beer until the game started or until the last game was played. It depended on who the batter was and what his tendencies were, but at two and two, with no fouls, I had the advantage. Sometimes to certain batters I pitched another inside pitch, and several times in that game that last pitch was fouled off for an out. Others who couldn't hit an outside pitch very well saw an outside strike coming and watched it go by for an out or hit it very weakly either back to me or second base. We ended up winning that game twelve to six. My plan worked perfectly. The third baseman played well, and they hit more balls to me than I care to count. That poor coach came in the next day clean as a whistle. We all had a good laugh, and truly, it was a lot of fun, and everyone took it as such. It was a good team-building exercise between the two teams, and we didn't even recognize it then, even if our company name was Recognition.

Every dog has his day and I had just had mine. The other coach quickly grew his beard back and it came time for round two. We bet facial hair again. Could my plan work two times in a row? The fact was I didn't even try. I figured they had me figured out and wouldn't fall for my tricks this time. I played my usual pitcher to start and hoped to stay close in score, but they got too far ahead. I switched in to pitch, and sure enough they had me figured out. They weren't falling for those tempting inside nonstrike pitches that day. I resorted to talking and pitching from the side of the mound, trying to distract them. I was doing all kinds of crazy stuff, but it wasn't working. They won something like sixteen to eight. They were good-natured about it and celebrated their win, and I was ordered not to shave my mustache. I said that a bet is a bet, but they said do not shave. I didn't. I came to work the next morning and walked into the front door, which led to the break room, and there was a barber chair sitting in the break room. That coach, in front of the entire production repair center, gave me a nice clean shave. It was all playful fun, and I played along. Who knew? I could be interviewing for something bigger in the future and not even know about it.

Pam had a good job at Walmart, and I had my job, so we had a little money rolling in. We always lived in an apartment in Irving, where we worked. We thought we could save a little money, so we moved to a mobile home community called Bunker Hill. We moved into a little cul-de-sac where Pam's best friend from high school lived with her son and boyfriend. I got to know my neighbor across the street well, and we became good friends. Truman was his name. He was height challenged, but that didn't bother him much since he could do a lot of different things very well. He was an especially good mechanic. He drank Budweiser for a while after work, then he'd grill a sirloin steak over coals for one-and-a-half minutes on one side, then flip, and one-and-a-half minutes on the other. The neighborhood would get together to watch the Dallas Cowboys, mostly at Truman's house. We had barbecues, water balloon fights, lots of fun. We didn't save any money though.

Pam and I tried to have children for many years. Pam tried all the tricks of the day to get pregnant, and finally I got checked. We found out that I was shooting only one barrel out of a double-barrel shotgun. I had surgery to fix that. We kept trying, and finally after six years, we were expecting. Our lives were turning on a dime suddenly, but we couldn't wait. We had waited long enough. Funny thing though. Pam tried every doctor's trick in the book, ovulation schedules, and different meds that do different things. I got fixed, but we continued with the treatments under doctors' orders. One day we decided to quit going to the doctor, and what happens happens, and we'll take what the Lord gives us if anything. It didn't take Him long, and He did not disappoint.

DID I MENTION I NEVER WAS A COWBOY?

I had a good friend at work named Chuck who happened to be gay. He wore Wrangler jeans and Wrangler shirts and cowboy boots, a real all-hat-no-cattle cowboy. Great guy though, and one of my best friends. He had a boyfriend, and they bought five acres about sixty miles from Dallas and put a mobile home out there, built pens and a little barn and bought two horses. Chuck asked me to come out and cook a brisket or two for a party for coworkers who were coming out from work on a Saturday. I got there to start up the fire. Chuck told me that he had this one horse that neither his boyfriend nor he could ride even though it was supposed to be broke. I was wearing a walking boot on one of my legs from tearing out the ligaments in my ankle from playing basketball at work, but what the heck, I'd give it a try. We saddled up the horse, I went to climb on and then, just as soon as I got a foot in a stirrup, he started jumping. I told Chuck the thing to do was to put him in the barn, fully saddled, and let him sweat for a couple of hours and tire him out. We tied him up in the tin barn, and we started drinking some beer. Folks started showing up. We all had plenty to drink, except for Pam, who was pregnant at the time. We ate, and we were all sitting on the back deck that late afternoon when I remembered that *horse*!

Chuck and I went to the barn, and he wasn't just sweated down; he was soaking wet. I wasn't ready to give up, so I took him out of the barn and put a foot in the stirrup. I got up in the saddle and thought, "It's about to get western." I walked him out of the gate, and sure enough he started bucking. I remembered quickly that I never was a cowboy no matter how much I tried. After two or three of the horse's jumps I fell off. In the process of humiliating me, he also tried to make me promise to never ride atop a horse again. While he jumped, he stepped on my inner arm, which, in the coming days, turned black and blue from my bicep to my wrist. He stepped on my lower back and on my neck, leaving a pretty nasty but thin cut about six inches long just below my ear to my Adam's apple. I was extremely lucky that the cut wasn't deeper.

I laid there, and one of my coworker's husbands came running down to help. Everyone else stayed on the deck and laughed. I didn't blame them. I was covered with dirt and bleeding, and my reputation as a south Texas cowboy was in question. I walked up to the house with my escort and walked into the house to get cleaned up. I came out of the bathroom and noticed a pump shotgun hanging over the bed in the bedroom. I thought, "I'm going to have fun with these folks." I pulled the shotgun off the wall, checked the chamber, and yes it was loaded—this was Texas after all. I went to the back door, slowly turned the doorknob to step out, and *boom*!!!! I shot a shell up into the air and pumped

another shell in. *Boom*!!! "Where's that fu$%&ing horse?"
I screamed. Chuck was screaming, *"Don't shoot my horse!"*
The folks were ducking and diving—I scared everyone
fairly good, and of course I wasn't going to shoot the
horse. By today's standards, it wasn't a safe prank to
pull, but back then it sure was funny.

ZEKE AND THE PRANK CALLS

Being a people watcher, I developed a little bit of ability to imitate people. One of the people I imitated the
best was Zeke, the shipping dock manager. He had a
lazy, whiny voice and didn't enunciate his words very
well, especially when he was laughing. Anyway, several
times a day, a shipping clerk, Diana, a Wannabe, trekked
down the hallway past our little corner window on her
way to shipping to do something or another. Thank
goodness there wasn't caller ID back then. One day,
with the urging of my coworkers, I called Diana while
imitating Zeke. I asked her in my best Zeke voice to
come to the dock and check on something. In a couple
of minutes, here she came walking by the window.
A couple minutes later, she walked back. If I recall
correctly, I had a mole in shipping, and he said she
came down and asked Zeke what he wanted, and he
said, "What are you talking about?" After going back
and forth denying a phone call, Diana walked back to
her office. I gave her ten minutes or so. I called back,
and then, in my best Zeke voice, I apologized, told her

I forgot what the problem was and just blanked out. "Can you please come down here?" Here she came down the hallway again. At this point Zeke thought, "She's losing her mind." She thought he was losing his. Perturbed at this point, she headed back to her office. I didn't wait long to call and, again in my best Zeke voice and my best Zeke laugh and explained that I was just messing with her and making her walk back and forth, but this time it was serious and I really needed her down there. This time I went down to the dock to witness what was going on. She came walking in and, well, I don't remember the exact cuss words she used, but she was not happy at this point, and she demanded to know what he wanted her for. Of course, he said he didn't call. She was livid, and he was so confused from this ass chewing that nobody could really understand what he was saying at this point because he was slurring so badly. I walked up and, in my best Zeke voice, said something like, "Hey Diana, come over here and look at this shipping label for me." Everybody roared with laughter, because by now everyone was in on the joke except for Zeke and Diana. They both wanted to kill me. Practical jokes and pranks are my specialty, besides wasting time. More practical jokes later.

Our lives changed forever with the birth of Melanie Rose. I think I speak for both of us when I say that Melanie was very easy to raise. It was a bit of a concern for both of us to learn that Mel was born hearing impaired. We didn't find out until she was about two, because she never talked. We got her hearing aids, and then she went off to the races. She adored books and Barney the Dinosaur. A couple years after Mel, Jennifer Mary was born. We moved to a duplex in the Colony, Texas, and by then we started to think about packing up and moving somewhere where we could raise our little family. I wanted to move south to somewhere around the coast area. Pam wanted to move back home to Kansas because she likes to witness the four seasons of Kansas instead of the one-and-a-half seasons that Texas has. So after moving up, down, sideways, and up again at Recognition, we both quit our jobs, cashed in our 401ks to have a little spending money, and moved to Kansas.

KANSAS

We moved to Kansas, Kingman to be exact, but when we first arrived, we stayed with my in-laws for a month. My mother-in-law was instrumental with helping us find a house to rent, not that she was in a hurry to get rid of her grandkids; she was just in a hurry to get rid of me. I'm kidding of course because my in-laws and I got along famously.

I was busy putting in applications, going to interviews, and finding out that I was starting again from entry level no matter what position I took. Wages were extremely low, and I couldn't find anything anywhere close to what

I was making in Dallas. I took a job at an iron foundry in another town in our county. It was a maintenance position, so I was part of a crew that repaired everything in the foundry. Now I never claimed to be a high society kind of guy, but we had a couple of yahoos that I swore just broke out of the joint and should go back. In the lunchroom there was a snack machine that didn't work. Someone kept it full of snacks and kept a money bag that you could deposit your payment in and make change if you needed to. We maintenance guys would take a later lunch than everyone else because we were fixing things while they were shut down for lunch. After production's lunch was over, these two guys would get the key and money bag, eat their fill out of the machine, and never put a dime in the bag. They would comb the fridge, see what was left in there, and swipe a thing or two out of it from time to time. That was blatant stealing, and I was an accomplice to it even though I didn't participate in it. Ride with an outlaw, die with an outlaw. That job was hot and dangerous, and I got out as quickly as I could. I had two close brushes with death, and two was too many for me.

CESSNA

I finally got a call from Cessna after applying there about ten months prior, and boy was I happy to get that maintenance job and leave the foundry. The manager of maintenance at the foundry, who I had a great deal of respect for, asked what he could do to keep me. I told him not much. I left and went to work on second shift at Cessna.

Cessna is an exceptionally large company, and we had a large share of characters in my department. Yes, they were funny, they wasted time joking and pranking, but these guys were smart as a whip, could do almost anything, and could work extremely hard, when they had to. It seemed though, we had a plethora of people named Steve who were the main characters in this comedy.

The first Steve I will write about, Steve One, was like a puppy dog—you couldn't kick him because he was so helpless. His job was to pick up hazardous waste containers and dispose of them properly. The thing about this Steve is that, when we sat around during breaks or lunch and had a conversation about something, most of the time Steve would not know anything about the topic. Talking about old cars with certain motors, countries overseas, types of iron—lots of topics guys would sit around and talk about—he would be quiet until the next day. I think on his time off the next day he would run to the library (this was before Google) and learn as much on yesterday's topic as he possibly could and then come into work and want to talk about yesterday's topic like he was an expert when the rest of us had moved on to a different one. I hate to admit it since, like I said, he was like a puppy dog, but I played pranks on this guy. I don't know how many times he would come driving up in his forklift for break or lunch or just find me working on something somewhere just to talk about when Chevrolet started putting a 350 cubic inch motors in their Camaros. If somebody distracted him, I would venture over to his forklift and turn off the gas. It had a propane tank mounted on the back end of the lift, and it had a valve that was supposed to be turned off if the lift was going to sit for an extended time. Steve would eventually climb aboard and take off driving. It had enough propane gas in the lines to run for about ten to fifteen seconds, and then the forklift would abruptly die. Repeatedly he would sit on that seat and crank that motor until it finally came to him that someone shut off his gas. He got off, gave us a little cussing, and turned his gas back on. I never understood after the first hundred times or so why after leaving us he would only make it ten seconds up the lane, it would die, and he would crank the motor for a while before figuring it out.

I worked on the roof a lot, and most roofs were rock, or I should say pebbles. Steve also drove a golf cart from time to time, and if I caught him driving by, I would pick up a pebble and try to hit his vehicle, which I did on a couple occasions. That pebble would hit the top of his cab, and he would slam on his brakes so hard that his head would hit the windshield. Luckily he was only going about ten miles an hour and his head was harder than the plastic windshield. Steve was something else.

One day another Steve, Steve Two, and I were changing filters in a paint booth. As we pulled the old filters out, which were like a 24 by 24 by 1 pleated filter, we promptly threw them like a frisbee down to the floor, and Steve One was down there to pick them up and box them for throwing away. It soon became a game of trying to throw these filters like a frisbee and hit Steve One with them. Now realize we were about thirty feet up in the air and about sixty feet from where Steve One was from us, so hitting him was very unlikely. But we were accurate enough that Steve One knew that we were tossing them in his direction. Our excuse was that we were trying to land them closer to him so he could pick them up without traveling all over the place. This wall was huge where these filters were—a good ninety feet across and thirty feet high with one filter after another after another taking up the entire wall space. It seemed like hundreds of filters were on that wall. I got down to the last one, the one all the way to the top and to the back of the booth. I went to throw it at Steve One, and, when I let loose of it, the filter caught some air, went upward into the ceiling, and knocked out a fuse link on a fire sprinkler head. Luckily Steve Two and I, being in a scissor lift, stayed dry, but unfortunately two thirds of these brand-spanking-new white filters we put in were now soaking wet and stained from being sprayed on by nasty, black fire line water. I was promptly called to the office that morning where my manager asked what happened. I wasn't lying when I told him it was the last filter of the day, and I was so happy that it was over that I had tossed it like a frisbee as hard as I could, and it had hit this fuse link. I never did mention I was really throwing it at Steve One.

RICK

Going to tell on myself now. When I was on third shift and worked midnight to seven in the morning, I would come over to the side of the roof where folks came into a turnstile to come to work. A big dumpster was right there next to the turnstile. There was a big light pointed down so walkers could see where they were going just below the rooftop. When I stood above it, nobody could see me. When it was time to come down and get ready to leave for the day on a couple of occasions, I would see that the dumpster was empty. I stood above that light with a few pebbles, and when someone who looked half asleep came through the turnstile, I would drop a rock into the dumpster from a forty-foot rooftop. Pop, pop, pop, around in circles the pebble went inside the trash dumpster. It scared the hell out of some of those people. I wish I had a video camera. Once, my friend and now my supervisor, Rick, was going to come in. Now Rick was one of the all-time greatest pranksters in Cessna history, so he had this coming. I had found a broken board from a pallet on the roof. It needed to come down anyway before it blew off and hit something important, but I had specific plans. Rick came walking through the turnstile, and I let him get a little bit of a head start to the shop when I tossed the board off to the empty dumpster. I made a bad toss! It hit the side of the dumpster and then careened off and slid on the ground right at Rick's feet! He jumped like a chicken on a hot plate. When the board came to rest, he looked up to the light I was standing above and said, "I can't see you, but I know you're up there you SOB." Rick was very jumpy, but he wasn't stupid.

I've known Rick for a long time. He was a maintenance guy just like me before he became a supervisor. I'd work with him sometimes. He had lots of stories of pranks he pulled on folks, so I didn't feel bad when I pranked him. He would regale me with stories of when he was on the Pawnee campus that is located on the southeast side of town. He found a crash test dummy that he used to play tricks with, like hanging him from a rope in an office hallway at night for the ladies to see when they came in in the morning. He also stood him up in a foyer with his hand raised above his head in a striking motion for an unknowing security guard to happen upon. Rick parked the truck at the gas pump for Cessna vehicles, put the hose in the gas tank, put the dummy in the driver seat, and rested his head against the window like he was sleeping. A line had formed and was waiting on his dummy to wake up. He drove through the building in a scooter one day with the dummy sitting on the passenger side, just as someone was walking up the aisle a fair distance away. Rick threw the dummy over the front of the scooter and ran him over. Folks from all over the area thought he really had run someone over. After that one trick the dummy had to go. Management had had enough. That's why I never felt bad about pranking him. I wasn't in his class though. I only tied the end of a hundred feet of caution tape to his back bumper and stashed the excess under his bumper for it to fall out while he was driving home.

The funniest, though, was when he was coming in on a Monday after being the on-call supervisor that weekend. I knew he would come stomping in with his laptop, books, on-call phone, just a lot of stuff in his hands—his arms were practically full. That night I went to his office, got my arm through the door, and pulled the bookcase in his office two feet away from the front of the door, then I locked it and closed it. Rick came in with a bunch of crap in his hands. I was peeking from down the hallway. He got to the door, tried to open it, and found it locked. He cussed a little as he never locked his door, but now it was locked for some reason and he had to hold all this crap in one arm so he could take out his keys. He unlocked the door and began to push his way in or, rather, kick his way in. He kicked the door with his first step holding all this crap. The door hit the bookcase and swung back hard and hits him back. Rick dropped all his stuff on the floor and started cussing bloody murder. I made my escape from being seen by Rick, but he knew who was responsible. Don't worry—he played plenty of tricks on me too. Pranking Rick was fun because he did take it well, but at first his eyes would get wide open, he gritted his teeth, and he had these cute little dimples that showed up on his cheeks. He left to go to another job in town, but I sure missed him when he left. He is an original.

STEVE THREE

Steve Three was another original. He had a most distinctive laugh that could be heard all over the plant. He was a mean prankster, willing to put the hurt on people because he was the strongest guy at Cessna. He never lifted weights; he was country strong, tall with big giant meat hooks for hands. When he put those claws into you, you were sure to come out with a bruise. I was on the passenger side of a pickup truck with another guy driving, and we had Steve in the middle. We thought we had him now, so we tried to grab him and put our own meat hooks into him for a change, but then he grabbed us both on the thigh and wouldn't let go. The doors flung open, and we tried to escape, but he wouldn't let go until we practically fell out, tearing his hands from our flesh. One on one was impossible with the behemoth. Two on one was impossible too. We finally got him one lunch time when we had three on one, and we had him pinned into the seat of a golf cart. He thrashed about and kicked, and I grabbed his legs below the knees and held them together while the other two tackled his upper extremities. I had the idea to pull off one of his shoes and began to tickle his socked foot. He howled with pain, and he was very ticklish. He thrashed about even harder and screamed, "I'm going to throw up!" I'm not that mean as to make a guy throw up, but I didn't let him off the hook and tickled him as appropriate, as he needed as much suffering as he put us through. One of the supervisors, Benny was his name, came walking in, stopped while watching us four wrestle inside a golf cart, then turned around and walked away. He didn't want to have to deal with the paperwork, plus he knew Steve Three deserved it as well.

Steve Two was another prankster, but he was a thinking man's prankster. Now stay close: this prank gets complicated. In our shop our work benches were side by side. They had sliding doors on top of the benches for storage of manuals and whatever else you wanted to store. These sliding doors had finger holes in them so you could slide them easily side to side. One night Steve Two caught a pigeon. Of course I was his accomplice. We decided to stick this pigeon into the storage area above Steve Three's bench. I tied a wire to the finger hole of that door, through the finger hole of the next door, and through the holes of the doors of the bench next to his and then onto mine. I pulled the wire and Steve's sliding door would open to reveal a pigeon that would flap his wings very hard and fly away, thus scaring the hell out of Steve Three.

Steve Two and I worked third shift, so we were alone before the next shift came in and set this up and made sure the doors worked perfectly. In the morning the first shift guys were coming in. Steve Three had a chair right in front of his bench, and he was later than his usual time to come in. A jumpy fellow sat in his chair. Steve Two and I decided to play the prank on this guy instead. I pulled the wire, the door slung open and hit with a bang, and the pigeon just sat there not doing a thing. That fellow jumped from just the slamming of the door opening, much less the bird sitting there staring at him, so he got up and left murmuring to himself. I closed the door and knocked on it to remind the pigeon to stay awake. Another unsuspecting guy sat down. I pulled the wire, the door slammed open, and...the stupid bird just sat there again. I closed the door and then banged on it pretty good trying to wake this pigeon up. As it turned out, Steve Three called in sick and never came to work that day. The pigeon was let loose to find some breakfast and a drink of water. This was an ill-conceived plan, poorly executed. We researched later that a pigeon will go instantly asleep in the dark. Who knew?

I know what you are thinking: does anyone get any work done? Why yes, we did. Rick, Steve Two, and Steve Three could work circles around most guys I ever worked with. They worked hard and played hard too.

HOME LIFE IN KANSAS

We lived in Kingman all our time since we moved to Kansas. Our kids went to St. Patrick's Catholic School and then moved on to Kingman High School. Our kids excelled in their own interests. Melanie loves music most of all and is very accomplished at the piano. Jennifer loves music as well, but she loved ballet and tap dance most of all. She participated in dance every year until she graduated from high school. I built her a wooden apparatus that had an old bicycle tube wrapped around it so she could stick her toes under the rubber to stretch her feet and shins out for pointe, which is what you see dancers doing when they sashay across the stage on their tippy toes. I never cared for ballet or tap until my daughter got into it. They call it an art, but I think it is more athletic. I always thought that if I were a football coach, I would have my players take ballet for stretching and strength training.

Our kids are good kids. No really, they were really, really good kids. Pam and I made it a point to sit down for our evening meal and eat together at the dining room table most of the time when there weren't band duties at ball games or dance class, in which case we may have as many as ten classmates to make fried pickles for. On weekends we generally ate breakfast together as well. One day Pam was preparing to make waffles with our waffle maker. She pulled down a box of some kind of mix. The box had a picture of pancakes on it. Melanie saw this and asked, "Isn't that a pancake mix?" Pam said this mix was a mix that could be used with all kinds of things. Melanie, in all her innocent wisdom, asked, "So all waffles are is pancakes in plaid?"

One day I went to the Pretty Prairie golf course, and Jennifer came along for the ride. They have a little ditch along number nine hole that is sometimes dry enough to at least not have standing water. It never dried up all the way, it seemed. When the standing water was gone, you could find a bunch of balls in there. One day I was holding onto a tree limb with my left hand and holding onto Jennifer's left hand while she was down in the ditch picking up balls and throwing them back up into the fairway behind me. We got a lot of golf balls that day. It has been said that a good day at the golf course is when you find more balls than you lose. It's also said that the older you get, the more you look for wayward golf balls. I'm not sure if it was that same day or not, but one time we were on the practice green, and both of us were practicing putting. I missed one and said I couldn't handle the pressure. She was ten years old or less, and she asked me what exactly the pressure was I felt. I explained that it's something that when you want something bad enough you get nervous about it and can't perform like you otherwise would and wind up missing the shot. I decided to give her a real-life lesson in pressure. I took a twenty-dollar bill from my wallet and laid it on the ground just beyond a hole in the green. I took the ball and backed away at least fifty feet and dropped the ball on the ground. I asked if she would like to win the twenty dollars. Of course she would. I told her to sink the putt and twenty dollars was hers, but can you handle the pressure? The putt had two breaks in it, virtually impossible. Jennifer studied it, lined up alongside the ball, and took a couple practice swings. She then backed off to putt, got behind the ball, and took another look. Study long, study wrong is a term we always say in golf, and Jennifer was studying long. She got alongside the ball again, the club went back and swung forward, and she struck it. It went up the first hill and broke the opposite way, then went up the second hill and broke off it the other way. I watched it all the way. It had good speed, it rolled well, and as it neared the hole, I thought, holy crap! The ball rolled right up to the hole, and it fell in. I picked up the twenty-dollar bill, gave it to her and told her she earned it. She handled the pressure. She told me she didn't feel any pressure because she had nothing to lose. She was wiser than the usual kid.

As the kids grew, our home was a home for all their friends as well. Both my kids had their own groups they ran with that were their age, and they did mix well, especially when they all got to high school. One thing our kids and their friends liked to play was treasure hunt. I would make up little clues that rhymed and give the first clue to the group, and it led to another clue somewhere else in the house where another clue was, and on and on and on until they found the prize, which usually was a stuffed animal or some kind of toy. Jen's friends consisted of Megan, who liked to be the boss and to make all the decisions. It's no wonder she grew up managing different stores in different states now. She was a born leader. Carlene was a happy one. She cherished her time with her friends. She did ballet and tap dancing with Jen. She was always upbeat and happy and cheering on whoever needed it. She had the kindest heart. Katie was next, the carefree one. She was fine with everything that anyone came up with. She just enjoyed the experience of friendship. Adam was another kid that hung out with this group. He was a kind and caring boy. These kids stayed at my house more than their own, it seemed sometimes, but it was OK with me. We played treasure hunt one afternoon, and I made up lots of clues. The four girls were over.

Megan would lead the charge to go wherever the clue led her. She was over at our house the most, and she knew our home very well. Carlene followed a close second and wanted to see and experience the chase. Katie would follow and laugh and talk the whole time. Jen was the ultimate host, glad her friends were having an enjoyable time. The chase of clues led them downstairs and back up again over and over. One of the clues led them downstairs to the shower. As the kids were upstairs, I made my way downstairs and hid behind the shower curtain. I heard the thunder of many little footsteps coming down the stairs, running around the corner and headed for the bathroom. They came in at full steam running and screaming, and, just as they got to the curtain, I pulled it back and gave a good scream! I scared the dickens out of them. Megan, in the lead as always, hit her head on a curtain rod and tore it off the wall. I felt bad about her hitting her head. When she was a little child, she had a bad concussion, and her head was susceptible to having more. I never scared them like that again, but it was fun the one time I did. It didn't stop Megan from leading the pack, however.

Melanie was the drum major in the band in her junior and senior years. She had a lot of the band over from time to time. They loved it when I made fried pickles. Lisa was Melanie's best friend and still is today. All these kids that I've mentioned are just like my own. I still enjoy seeing them now and then when they come to town.

Over the years I've heard lots of noise in our house, but it was a joyful noise, and I loved every minute of it, and Pam did too. Melanie constantly played her saxophone, sometimes so much that she would forget to do her homework. She also loved to play the piano and took lessons for all her growing-up years. She became an exceptionally talented player and played for all the students who wished to sing in the school talent shows and such. She and Lisa teamed up a lot of times through the years. Mel also played in church and still does. She studied piano in college as well. Jenn took piano lessons for a while, but she really excelled at tap and ballet. She loved it so much that she would just start tap dancing to the music in her head. We had hard wood floors and a linoleum floor in the kitchen. I would be doing the dishes or cooking something, and Jenn would regale me with a story of the day and her feet were constantly moving, tapping, and dancing. She would even tap while standing in line at the grocery store.

Like all children, they grow up and go on to make their own way. When Melanie was a senior in high school, she was all ready to go to Kansas State University. I thought she didn't look at enough colleges, so I encouraged her to look around. I received a phone call out of the blue from a representative from a school in Iowa called Briar Cliff University. I convinced her to look, so we planned a road trip to Sioux City to visit. It was eight hours away, but when we visited it seemed like a good fit, so she decided to attend BCU. When she graduated from high school, we threw her a party. I wanted to give her something special just from me. I decided to write a poem, or something that resembles a poem, that was about her life growing up in our home. It's called "Words and Memories."

WORDS AND MEMORIES

Words cannot describe what you mean to me.
I could write for years, and I will not be
Finished with my words that would collect and like
A series of books, like an encyclopedia,
The memories of your young life come to me like churning clouds,
Feelings of joy, happiness, a little frustration, but always proud.
I remember your sad face every day when I left you at the sitter's.
I drove down that road many times, my heart feeling guilty and bitter.
I remember things you don't because you were too young, but
I'd bounce you on my knee singing a song,
And you would laugh and bring joy and laughter to your Mom and me.
It really does seem like it was just yesterday,

I remember it so vividly.

I remember boo-boos, a broken arm, lost teeth,
learning to ride a bike,

Birthday parties, skating, learning to bat a ball, to
throw a strike.

I remember snow sledding in the driveway, calling
each other floppers.

Picking green beans and potatoes, going fishing, and
catching grasshoppers.

I remember reading books over and over,

Tikki Tikki Tembo and *I'll Love You Forever.*

I remember making up bedtime stories off the top
of my head,

Then tucking you snugly and safely into your bed.

I remember a trip to the hospital,

Your Mom took you with a very dry cough and you
could barely breathe.

I stayed home with your sister, we waited patiently
for a call.

The call finally came, your Mom said you wanted me.

I packed up your sister and her things and
came immediately.

They put you in a tent covering you in the bed,

You wanted me to climb in the tent with you, which
I did.

I laid there next to you in the hospital bed getting
dripping wet

From the humidifier that pumped moisture inside.
I didn't care, I wanted to stay by your side because
you wanted me there.
I did nothing to help you get better, but you made
me feel
Like I was the most important doctor in the hospital
that day.
I remember songs, the saxophone and piano playing
in the air.
The neighbors told me they wanted you to
keep playing,
They wanted to hear the melodies that you played
over and over.
I remember the Christmas plays, band concerts,
Football and basketball games,
I'd look over to the band to see you directing
the notes.
I'd be so proud; I couldn't let the crowd see the
Moisture gathered in my eyes.
Damn, how time flies.
I remember talking to you.
Trying to prepare you to go out in this world.
And wondered if I did a good enough job as a dad.
Did I give you the right words? and if you are glad
that I care enough to bore you this bad.
We tried to teach you to care for others and to love
God and Trust in his will.
You were a straight-A student for us,

But still tried to instill
In you that family is the most important thing to you
next to God.
Melanie, you will be successful in anything you want
to achieve.
I wanted you to be independent but still can't help
but be selfish—
I want you to go for you but stay for me at the
same time.
Letting go is harder than I ever thought it would be.
Trying to come up with my own words to tell you
how much I love you,
I find I have to steal the words
From one of favorite books of all time:
I'll love you forever, I'll love you for always,
As long as I'm living my baby you'll be.

Melanie graduated from BCU with a bachelor of
arts in English and a minor in piano and now lives in
Wisconsin, where she lives happily with her husband,
Dan, three daughters, and one son on the way. The
saxophone is gone, but you still hear tinkling ivories
from a piano from her and her students. One day we'll
hear our grandchildren playing on it.

Jen was in the National Honor Society, is a pub-
lished author, and danced until she graduated from
high school. She choreographed her own solo dance,
which she entitled "Rosann," in honor of her grand-
mother who had just passed away that past winter.

Grandpa was a wheat farmer. He was a small family farm operator and had older equipment. My brother-in-law bought what I guess we could call an antique, a 1955 John Deere model 55 combine. It ran like a top and still does to this day. With dual tires it can cut wheat and drive through standing water depending on the size of the load in the bin. My nephew Jacob and I drove it down to Grandpa's, about a forty-mile trip, going fifteen to twenty miles per hour. It didn't have a cab on it, so getting a suntan was easy that day. Jacob drove it for years during harvest and did a fantastic job, but it was time for him to leave and go to college and have other things to do. Grandpa worried about who would drive the '55, or the "Green Steed," as it was aptly named. Jennifer was dying to try, and I told him so. Grandpa was a bit old-fashioned and believed in the theory that genders had their place, but as he got older and watched Pam and my sister-in-law Brenda drive the wheat trucks back and forth to town with a load for years, he was slowly changing his mind. I took Jen out, gave her thirty minutes of instruction, and let her go by herself. By late in the afternoon, talking about his little granddaughter operating that old dusty combine made him cry. He was so happy that Jen was able to do it, but more importantly wanted to do it, wanted to work the land. Grandpa had a little field by the road. Semi trucks would come by with grain trailers heading from their fields into town to drop off their loads and back to the fields to fill them again. More than once I could hear their motors wind down to slow a little bit. I couldn't figure out if they were slowing down to look at that old combine in the field or the cute blond operating it. Probably both. It came time for Jennifer to graduate from high school, and due to what she wanted to major in, her choices were limited. She decided on Wichita State University. Like for Mel, I wrote her a poem for her high school graduation.

A BEAUTIFUL NOISE

Pitter patter back and forth through our
home's doors,
Tap, tap, tap, resonating on the auditorium's floor.
Life's a dance, a song once said,
Your life's a beautiful noise going through my head.
Curly Scooter, Grandpa once called you,
Endless curls and endless smiles were abound.
Your heart was always larger than your little body,
Leaving endless smiles on those that you
were around.
A child of curiosity, studying bugs, climbing trees,
Christmas time at Mema's, picking pecans on
your knees.
Summer times big slugger, a huge swing of the bat,
Tender hugs and lots of pets for a friendly stray cat.

Many years of plodding up and down the dance
center stairs,
Many years Mom and I sat in a car waiting under the
moon's glare.
Coming home and climbing into your bed,
"Good night and I love you" is a beautiful noise
inside my head.
Quite often you helped me with the Knights,
Peeling potatoes or installing new lights.
The conversations we had while our work was
being done,
It's a beautiful noise with a little work and a lot
of fun.
You'd play your clarinet as often as you pleased,
And the piano too, wonderful notes and a soft touch
of the keys.
Some days music could fill our home from morning
till bed,
It's a beautiful noise going through my head.
A radio blaring as you take a bath.
With little time left for English and math.
And singing songs while you had your
headphones on,
It's a beautiful noise I can listen to from dusk
till dawn.
Shuffles and taps coming from ballet and tap shoes,
I've often wondered how many pairs you have had.
Would they have filled a closet or two?
Knowing it all comes to an end makes me very sad.

Your dance has come full circle, as you started
dancing pointe,
With blisters on your toes and aches in every
single joint.
You worked through it and never worried about
your plight,
As Candy Land dancers and the Scarecrow danced
through the night.
You directed the pep band during basketball games;
Keeping time with your hands as they announced the
players' names.
It was a beautiful noise as the crowd cheered aloud,
As you struck up the band after seeing a time out.
Jennifer, you are our baby,
We didn't leave anything to chance,
For you are our beautiful noise,
Our wonderful song and our graceful dance.
Jennifer, I love you, and I am so proud of you.
As you proceed to your next endeavor,
Your dance, your songs, your beautiful noise
Will be with me forever and ever.

Jennifer graduated from WSU with a bachelor of
science in laboratory sciences. She lives in Wichita and
married her high school and grade school sweetheart,
Blayn. Their kids, two dogs named Chell and Bailey,
should consider themselves incredibly lucky to have
doggy parents who are animal lovers like them.

LONGHORNS IN THE ROAD

Our girls grew up with Grandma and Grandpa being a very big part of their lives. I always felt that my parents were shortchanged a bit, especially since my two girls were my folks' only granddaughters—the rest were grandsons. We still went to visit at least twice a year and stayed a week or more when we went. On occasion when we vacationed in Texas, I would be asleep in the morning and there would be a knock on the bedroom door. It would be my dad waking me up to help him with some kind of chore he needed help with. I wanted to scream, "*I'm on vacation*!!!" when this would happen, but truly, my dad wouldn't ask for help if he didn't need it.

On one such occasion, we were driving out toward the family farm in Koerth, and as we drove he explained that the day before he had bought a longhorn cow and calf. After they were loaded in the trailer, he took off for the farm. As he drove down the road, he noticed in the rearview mirror that one of the cows' big horns seemed to be sticking out of the back of the trailer. He checked the other mirror and saw that the back end of the gate was wide open! He panicked a bit and put the brakes on a little too hard, and eventually, after much confusion on the parts of the cow and the calf, both fell out of the back of the trailer. The calf quickly weaseled his way in between barbed wire and into someone's pasture.

The mom couldn't follow. Dad pushed the cow with his pickup the last mile or so to the farm. Of course the cow was not happy being separated from her baby.

That morning Dad brought me along to get that baby. We parked on the side of the road and met my brother-in-law Jerome there. We got out on foot with ropes to catch this little booger. I was thinking we could call the owner of the pasture and pin him up, but I'm not a cowboy, so what did I know? I forgot who officially roped the calf, but the rope was quickly in my hands, and I dragged the calf over to the fence and pulled him under the bottom wire. This calf fought and pulled, and I was worn out in the early morning Texas heat and humidity, which on a clear sunshiny day could feel like it was above 97 percent. As I pulled and fought and cussed that poor calf, my dad and brother-in-law had a fun time standing there laughing at me. I finally got the rope inside the trailer, wrapped it around one of the bars and pulled him in. Now come to find out that Jerome had ideas of buying this cow and calf. He had a nice longhorn herd of his own and was going to add to it with this nice pair. He told my dad to leave the cow at the farm for a couple of weeks, and he'd be able to pick them up after they settled down. Dad and I hauled the calf to the farm and let it go, and the mom came running up instantly and had a family reunion. Dad said, "Let's get them pinned up, loaded up, and take them over to Jerome's." I reminded him that Jerome didn't want them for a couple weeks and to allow them to settle down. Dad said he didn't want these crazy longhorns in his pasture either. We got all the cattle to come running to the pens coaxed with a little feed. I remember two bulls, a Brahma and a Charolais, loping side by side. As they came through the gate together, the Charolais hip checked the Brahma right into a corner post at the gate and bent that post over sideways, which loosened the whole fence. I thought, "Great, another chore to take care of."

Don't ask me how—it may have been angelic forces at work here—but we got the cow and the calf separated from the rest of the herd fairly easily. Dad was trying to back the trailer up to the chute and having little success. I felt like hollering at him, "Need some help greenhorn?"—a term I heard lots of times growing up. I decided against the notion of saying that though. As Dad was trying to back the trailer up, the cow was getting crazy, running back and forth across the pen and trying to jump it a couple of times. The pen was sturdy and close to six feet tall, so the cow didn't have any success in getting out. My dad, still lining up the trailer, hollered, "Get in there and calm her down!"

This time I was able to reply, "You get in there and calm her down with those big-ass horns."

Finally the trailer was in place, somehow we got the cow and calf in the trailer, and we took off down the road. We pulled into Hellscrook Haven, which is Jerome and my sister Jocelyn's place. Dad backed up to Jerome's pen, and we unloaded the cow and the calf. We stopped at the house on our way out to talk to my sister, since this was the first time I'd seen her in a few months. Jerome came driving up and asked, "Why are you guys here?" Dad told him we had dropped off the cow. Jerome said, "I said I don't want that cow here." He walked down to the pen because my dad's pickup and trailer were blocking the lane, preventing him from driving to it. A minute later we heard Jerome scream back up to the yard, "Get this damn cow! She's tearing up my pen! I told you I don't want that cow here!" We went back down there with the pickup and trailer and loaded her up again. Jerome now had a job, as some of his boards on his pen were broken due to the cow going crazy. We took off down the road, and I asked, "Dad where are you taking this cow to now?" He said he was taking her to the auction sale in Gonzalez, which had an auction every Saturday. He dropped me off at home and proceeded on to Gonzalez without me. Later he came home and said he made money on that cow and calf. Funny, whenever talking about horse trading and wheeling and dealing with my dad, he never lost any money. All the trouble we'd gone through that day, no amount of money would have been a profit in my estimation. The way I saw it, he should have had labor cost because I should have been on the payroll that day.

LET'S HAVE AN AUCTION!

My mom and dad came to Kansas to visit one year. They drove my mom's car, a big four-door Chrysler Fifth Avenue. We lived in town, and I thought my dad was not going to have a good time just sitting around doing nothing. He had a tough time sitting around. He couldn't sit down and watch TV very much, maybe a sitcom, and he sure didn't have the patience to watch a movie. There was a horse-and-mule auction going on in town that weekend. On Friday they sold lots of tools, antiques, horse-pulled wagons—anything could be found there. I decided that the auction was the place to go and the perfect pastime for my dad, and boy was it ever. When my mom and dad packed up to go home, the entire back seat and trunk were taken up with all kinds of stuff that he had bought. He enjoyed the horse-and-mule sale so much that the next time it was held, he came back with a friend, and both were driving a truck and a trailer. They bought Belgian mules, and Dad's friend bought a wagon. We had to take the wheels off, lay the wagon across the bed on his friend's pickup sideways, and tie it down so that the wagon could make it back to Texas. His friend bought it only because he thought he was just driving the price up higher, and then he got stuck with the bid. I guess it could have made a fine yard ornament or playhouse for my kids in our yard if we didn't find a way to load it up. Dad had a big load of crap in the back of his truck. He also bought a couple of "big jacks," or maybe tall donkeys is a better description. He thought Kansas had the biggest jackasses he had ever seen. Of course I'm talking about donkeys here. He had the idea to cross them with the smaller donkeys you find in Texas to make a medium-size donkey, I guess, which would bring more money than the little donkeys. I thought, fine, but why not buy a tall male and female donkey and haul them back and sell the tall offspring of them? What did I know?—I'm not a cowboy.

He told me on one of my later trips to Texas that the load of stuff that was in the back of his pickup was never unloaded. He sold it all from the back of it pieces at a time and made money on everything. I remember he bought a boxful of new hammer handles for a dollar for the box. He said he sold every one of those handles for just a dollar each. That big box had to have at least a hundred handles in it. He said most folks wanted five or ten. That's my dad, a real wheeler-dealer, a real horse trader in every sense of the word. I'm not sure whatever became of the great jackass breeding expo that was supposed to be held, however.

MOM AND DAD

My Mom always worked a job until she was well into her eighties. She worked in a leather factory making, sewing, and staining all manner of western leather equipment from saddles to bridles and even belts and wallets. She was a very accomplished seamstress, and after she retired from the factory in her sixties, she sewed all manner of clothing, from hemming pants and shirts to making bridesmaid dresses and probably a wedding dress or two—or the alterations at the very least.

When we went to visit a couple times a year, she would tell folks she was on vacation while we were there, but she still had some customers stop by and pick up stuff she had done for them. Sometimes she couldn't help but do a little business while we were there. In Texas people get a little crazy about their weddings and have four, five, or nine bridesmaids. When she did alterations, she needed the bridesmaids there to measure and such, and getting them all there at one time or another usually required weekends when the girls were home from college. She always took them back to her back sewing room. I often thought that I should make her a sign to hang on her wall saying alterations cost money, but altercations are free. My mom was so nice she never had an altercation except maybe with Dad. As she got older, she quit sewing due to her body pains, but she still enjoyed quilting and even took to teaching her grandniece.

My brothers, sisters, and I decided to throw mom an eightieth birthday party. We rented the American Legion hall in Sweet Home. We were going to have our old neighbor and his son play their accordions, and my cousin Jeff on the drums, and my uncle Linwood on the guitar. Uncle Linwood was an accomplished guitarist. He played probably in every polka and country band around the area at some time or another. He was always after me to come up and sing when we were attending an event he was playing, even though I can't sing a lick. I had an idea about a song or a poem for Mom for quite some time. I was going to have Melanie produce a melody for it, but we never got around to it. I wrote it, and unfortunately I was the only one from the family from Kansas to make it to the party. The night before the party, I was with Mom watching TV, and I told her I was going to get some gas in the car so I wouldn't have to do it tomorrow before the party. I quickly drove to Uncle Linwood and Aunt Joanne's house down the road a bit. I read the song to them, and they thought it was good. I asked Uncle Linwood if we could come up with a melody, kind of like "Streets of Bakersfield" by Dwight Yoakam. My cousin Leanna was there as well; she pulled it up on her phone for my uncle to hear. He instantly picked it up with his guitar, we practiced a time or two, and we had it down just like that. Now I know how a real musician does it. The next day was the party. Everyone had a wonderful time and a great meal, and then it was time for the band. In the middle of the concert, I jumped up to sing my song and immediately retired afterward. I was a one-hit wonder. It was called "Mama Time and Apple Strudel."

I've been to a lot of places, chasing dreams like fireflies,

Some I've hit on, some I've missed on, some I let them pass me by.

But one place my mind goes back to, no matter where I may roam.

Give me some stew and a Shiner beer, a place in Texas called Sweet Home

Chorus

To see my Momma in the kitchen, rolling dough with a pin.

She ain't making no chicken and noodles, want my momma time and apple strudel.

You know a boy needs his momma to help make the world slow down.

And I can almost taste her cooking before I even hit the town.

Chorus

Now you know I love folks everywhere, please don't take me wrong.

But this old boy loves his mama, enough to make me write a song.

Chorus

I'd trade the whole kit and caboodle for some mama time and apple strudel.

I'm still waiting for my Grammy. I know it's not very good, but it came from the heart and Mom loved it as well as my family. I got an A for effort. She had a wonderful time with old friends at her eightieth birthday party, as well as her eighty-fifth, and now her ninetieth she had last year. The band didn't get to strike it up the last two because of various reasons,but Mom had lots of fun and memories, nonetheless. Her great grand-daughter Lainee played on her guitar and sang "Can't Help Falling in Love" by Elvis Presley at the ninetieth party. The music never stops with the family.

Dad passed away on July 25, 2005, when he was seventy-six years old. He had dementia and had developed allergies to almost everything outside that he had worked around his entire life, and it really slowed him down. He was living in a nursing home for about two years. One day when we were in Texas, Jocelyn and Jerome were hosting one of their many BBQs that I had come to expect when I was down there. I stopped at the nursing home, picked up Dad, and drove him to my sister's house. He used a walker to get around and moved slowly. He was as used to these BBQs as I was, so he sat down on a chair on the gravel driveway like we always did. Like I mentioned before, Dad liked to drink beer in his day, but he had since quit when he went into the nursing home. If it bugged him to quit, I didn't notice on my trips. Jerome and I were both enjoying a beer, and I asked Jerome if he thought it would be OK if Dad had one. Jerome agreed that one couldn't hurt so he asked, "Daddy, do you want a beer?"

Dad replied, "Well hell yes." So we gave him a Bud Light, and he drank it down in no time and threw the can in the driveway. I looked at Jerome with a "whaddya think?" look, and he said sure, so I asked Dad if he wanted another. Sure he did, and he drank that one with a lot of gusto as well and tossed the can. We waited and talked it over about the possibility of a third. Our discussion said one more and that's it, because we're not sure how beer works in relation to his meds, and besides it's about time to pack it all in and head inside to eat. We asked again, and he agreed one more should suffice. He drank this one more slowly, deliberately, like he was savoring this one when he devoured the two before. When it was time to go in to eat, he chugged the rest, tossed the can high in the air, got up out of his chair, and walked up the steps to the back of Jerome's house and into the door, forgetting all about the walker. Jerome and I just laughed about it. I'm not saying he was 100 percent cured of whatever ailments he had, but we knew he felt better if he could just have a drink every so often.

Often when we had these little parties, we would play dominoes after the meal. You know how to play dominoes. You play numbers up against like numbers and try to make all the ends add up to a sum that is a multiple of five. The way I play the game is not rocket science, but the old-timers like my dad, and Jerome as well, knew a little bit more about the finer points of the game. Winning a game only led to having bragging rights for a minute, then it was on to the next game. The fun part was to listen to these folks talk. "Fit teen" was screamed when someone scored fifteen points. Nickels and dimes took the place of fives and tens. If I were ever lucky enough to score twenty-five, I would declare "motorboat," a term I picked up from playing dominoes with Slipfoot Wilson at Recognition Equipment.

After the dominoes were shuffled, everyone picked their "rocks" and declared they picked the worst ones ever and they were not going to be worth a damn this hand. Dad said something every time he had you in a pickle, like knowing he forced you to have to pass or at least not score. He'd grin a little and say, "Whattaya gonna do now, shoot ducks?" I never knew where that came from, and I didn't care to hear when I was playing behind him. I say it till this very day though, and I even say it when I see folks having a tough time doing or deciding anything. I get those looks like what the hell does that mean? I don't bother explaining; I just laugh at the memories and wish he could look me in the eye one more time and say, "Whattaya gonna do now, shoot ducks?"

JOE AND ROSANN

My in-laws both passed away in 2013, Rosann on January 1 and Joe on October 14. I already mentioned that they were wheat farmers. There was no telling what Joe might say at times. We called his little sayings "Joeisms." These days, when the opportunity arises and we remember a Joeism that relates to the situation, we say like there is a numbered like a list of Joeisms, which there isn't, but there should be. A good example of this is Pam looking at the clouds and wondering aloud about the possibility of rain. I would reply, "Joesism number twenty-two, those are come-and-go-party clouds." Or I would say, "Joeism number twelve, those are fuzzy scare-tactic clouds." What's the difference between come-and-go-party clouds and fuzzy scare-tactic clouds? Your guess is as good as mine, but Joe knew the difference between them. Maybe if you were to pick on me, I would say, "Joeism number seven, you're breeding a scab on your nose." There's a bunch of them, and I had better write them down when someone in the family says one of them so they are not forgotten. One time we were playing the game Scattergories. It's the game where you are given a letter, and you have to answer a list of questions with a word that begins with that letter. If you answered the question with an answer no one else in the game produced you earned a point. Joe wasn't particularly good at the game, and I'm not sure he was enjoying it. One round, the letter was M and one of the questions was a pair of something. We all racked our brains. Now without the timer going, I can think of mittens or muck boots right off the top of my head, but that day I came up with nothing, and I think most of the other players didn't have an answer either. We all assumed Grandpa didn't have a word either, but we asked just to be nice. I guess it was the company around him—too many female grandchildren—but he said sheepishly, "Mammary glands, but that's not very good." Oh crap, we just fell about the place! That was quite a laugh he brought on. Only Grandpa could come up with that one.

For a time I worked nights from midnight to seven. Joe would call me the day before or early in the morning and ask if I could come down and help him repair something or another. I didn't always make it just that day, but I often did. Many times I told Rosann when I showed up, I won't be staying for lunch so don't make any extra for me. She never listened. I was always there until she called for lunch at about eleven thirty so we could eat and Joe could catch the latest news on TV. First I must tell you that like most grandmas, Rosann could cook great, and my personal favorite of her recipes was scalloped potatoes. She made the potatoes just at the right texture, and the cheese would be slightly brown on the edge of the potatoes. It was my firm belief that she made the best scalloped potatoes in the world. Every time I told her not to make any lunch for me, she did, and she would make her famous scalloped potatoes. How could I pass that up? I think she was proud of her ability to make them without a recipe, as she should have been because they turned out great every time. I was not the only one who thought they were the best either. When it was time to leave, I would get Joeism number three, which was "Thanks a lot till you're better paid." I was well paid in scalloped potatoes.

Rosann got ovarian cancer and spent quite a bit of time in the hospital. She lost a lot of physical strength while she was there. I'd come to visit and give her a little bit of guff. "What are you doing lazing around?" or "Get up and make me some scalloped potatoes." I'd accuse her of being a lollygagging lollygagger on other days and some other wise cracks, but it was always followed up with "Make me some scalloped potatoes." She finally left the hospital after more than forty days, and then she stayed in our home with us for a period. Pam got her up to walk around the circle we had around the wall between our kitchen and living room—do some laps is what Pam called it. Rosann worked some of her strength back but never was the same as before the cancer. One day after all that grief I gave her, she mustered up the strength to make some scalloped potatoes. OK, she made them for everybody, but I think with me giving her hell all the time, I enjoyed them the most. She did return home to the farm for a year or so before things went south for her again.

Most folks say they don't get along with their in-laws very well. Mother-in-law jokes have to come from somewhere, but they didn't come from me. I was one of the incredibly lucky ones. I had a good relationship with my in-laws. I miss them terribly.

AN
UNWANTED VISITOR

So far, my book has been light and, I hope entertaining in a humorous way. That is going to change. I play golf with about six or seven regular friends, but there are three of us who play a lot of tournaments, and we pick an extra player out of the rest of the bunch to make a foursome. In September of 2020, we got in a tourney in Hesston, Kansas. We really didn't enjoy the tourney so much because it was raining, and the temperatures dropped down close to fifty degrees. When we arrived the weather was nice, but it didn't last long. I was having the worst day of my life. My clubs had old grips on them, and when they got wet I had to squeeze them with every ounce of energy to keep them from flying out of my hands and down the fairway. But besides the rain, wind, and cold, I was feeling very dizzy when I went to putt. I am usually a good putter, but this day I missed everything by a wide margin. I would look down and study my line, take a couple of practice swings to try to get the speed of the club correct, and then it would hit me: dizziness.

It happened on a few drives off the tee as well. I got to where I was swinging and totally missing the ball, which to beginners isn't a hard thing to do, but I hadn't done that in years. Luckily I never fell. I learned two things quickly: don't stare down to the ground too long, and if I did, look up at the horizon and it will go away in a few seconds. A pitiful day and a pitiful effort by me. I went to my doctor, and she thought it was vertigo. I also had a bad bout with hiccups. They would often start and not stop for a while, and it had nothing to do with eating or drinking. I have had vertigo before when I was helping my daughter Jenn move one day; I picked up a heavy box of books and threw the box up onto my shoulder, and it wound up slamming me in the ear. This felt different.

As usual I wanted to lose a few pounds that summer, and I lost about thirty quickly. I took blood pressure meds, but my pressure would differ a lot when I took it sitting down versus standing up, which was also beginning to make me dizzy just standing there. My doctor thought that maybe with losing thirty pounds I didn't need to take as much blood pressure meds, so we cut them in half or a while. I still worked and felt fine most of the time, and on September 29, things took a wild turn.

I was headed home in our silver Impala that we got from Pam's folks after they both passed. I was driving west on a two-lane road, and on the north side of an intersection a white Chevy sedan was stopped at a stop sign. I didn't have a stop sign, so I was just cruising right along when, at the last possible second, the white car started to go into the lane I was driving in. It all happened so fast. I'm sure I applied the brakes, but it didn't help much at all. I remember having enough time to think, "This is it. This is where my story ends." I was going at least sixty or just below because of the brakes, and the Chevy was barely moving. What do you do? I didn't have time to think or look at the situation, so I did what I always told myself to do if and when a deer jumped out in front of me: just run him over, keep the car headed in a straight line, and keep all four tires on the ground. I walloped that car. The front of his car was pointed south before the wreck but was in the ditch and pointed northwest by the time I was done with it.

My crash bag went off and knocked my glasses off my face, and the car filled up with smoke. I quickly did an inventory of my body, and everything seemed OK, so I felt around on the floor and found my glasses at my feet and my phone on the passenger-side floor. I had survived. A knock on the window came from a nice guy who worked at Cessna as well, but I didn't know him. He was driving behind me at a distance. He asked if I was OK, and I told him I thought so. He and another fellow went over to the other car and checked on its passengers in there. It happened to be an elderly couple who was vising the area from Arizona and was driving their niece's car.

I got out and started to direct traffic, as this was a two-lane road and my car was taking up one of them. I called Pam and told her of my wreck; my right arm was bruised from the air bag, and my upper back was feeling the strain of the wreck. I was shaken but had to give myself something to do, and directing traffic while on the phone with a swollen forearm was just the ticket to get my mind right.

A sheriff showed up and then a fire truck as well as an ambulance. I answered questions and filled out an accident report. I had just had back fusion surgery the past December, and I was worried that the wreck might have screwed something up, so when I was asked if I needed medical attention, I said yes. These folks were at fault, and they had insurance, so what the heck. Let's make sure my fusion was still fused. My neck and upper back ached too, and I knew that as soon as the adrenaline wore off and I woke up the next day, I may have more trouble than I had now. It's better to be safe than sorry.

The first ambulance took the older couple away. They never said a word to me, although we were in each other's presence. The husband had been driving, and he could walk but seemed a little dazed and confused. His wife, however, looked fine and was madder than an old wet hen. I waited for another ambulance to show up. I sat on the bumper of the fire truck and apologized to the firefighters for getting them out there. One of the firefighters said not to apologize, it's what they do. I said I would rather they be at the station watching the Ellen DeGeneres show or some other daytime talk show that was on TV during that time of the day. That made them all have a hearty laugh.

My ambulance showed up and I climbed up the steps and sat down in a chair. The paramedic said it was his chair and that I had to lie on the gurney. I was beginning to think that maybe this was a bit of overkill and a waste of my fellow taxpayers' money. They strapped me in, and we found out via the radio that there was an accident on the main road through Wichita, Highway 54 or Kellogg—it's called by both names. We drove through neighborhoods to get to Wesley Hospital on the east side of town. I chose to be taken to Wesley because our youngest daughter Jennifer, works there as a lab technician. I just wanted her close by if need be.

We finally arrived, and Pam nearly beat me there

from our little hometown driving through the wreck on 54 and all. They gave me a little space in between curtains, took my vitals and all that, and took me to get a CAT scan of my neck and back.

Now this was during the time of COVID, and I was surprised how fast everything was going. I got the scan and was lying on a hospital bed; someone came in, an ER doctor, and told me that my neck and back looked fine but they saw a growth of some sort on the upper end of where my neck goes into my brain. I thought, yep, that is a bit of calcium that affected my softball swing when I was forty, and now going on fifty-five, it affects my golf swing. I can swing, but not as fast as I possibly can. It will leave my neck stiff and unmovable for a few days if I try to swing a club hard. But still they wanted to do an MRI to get a better look and try to determine exactly what it was. Better safe than sorry, I suppose. So then I got wheeled down to the MRI room to get a better look. Afterward I was back in my room with Pam when another doctor came in. OK, I'm almost out of here now I thought. She told me that I had a tumor on the base of my spinal cord and my brain. She said a whole lot more, but I really did not hear much after the word tumor. I'm thankful Pam was there to listen and ask questions. She told us this tumor was called a grade two ependymoma and is the rarest type of brain tumor, especially in adults. There are only about two hundred a year in the US. It usually gets misdiagnosed because it is so rare, so the survivor rate is not great, but if caught early enough, it is treatable. I'm not quoting the doctor, just quoting Google, because I had plenty of time to do some research on it.

I thought I had seen my death coming in the form of a car accident, and now I heard the two words, brain tumor, and I could see my death coming slowly and painfully. I questioned myself: which was better or worse, for death to come quickly or to come slowly? To this day I still have not made up my mind.

But as we sat there waiting for a neurosurgeon to show up, we decided that maybe I was the recipient of a miracle—a tumor that gets misdiagnosed most of the time, and mine is not only not misdiagnosed but found early. A neurosurgeon came in and was highly informative and answered all our questions, although I do not remember most of them. I remember her saying that this tumor looked old and was probably benign but no guarantees yet. The surgeon was a young gal, maybe forty tops, and I may make her mad with that guess. She said she never performed surgery to remove an ependymoma but would like to do it, or I could go anywhere else I chose to.

I really didn't even think about it much. I could have gone to Mayo, or Houston, or found the surgeon who is the foremost expert on these types of tumors. I liked this surgeon's confidence, her way of talking about these things. I wanted to stay close to home in case things went badly. I decided at once while she was talking with me to go with her even though she was young and had never performed this surgery before. Thinking about it now, I must have taken a knock on the head from that car wreck. This was all on a Wednesday night, and the surgery was scheduled for Friday. They just kept me in the hospital until then. I had lots of time to think about it all. I thought from time to time, "Why me?" but it was usually followed up with "I'm glad it's me and not my wife or one of my kids or grandkids." Still I also had the feeling that I was blessed to have this found in this way. I could have gone a long time with a vertigo diagnosis until it was too late like most folks with this kind of tumor. All my friends were shocked. One day I was at work, the next I was having surgery on my brain.

On Thursday night my surgeon had an emergency surgery on somebody and was not well rested enough to do mine. I was rescheduled for the upcoming Wednesday and discharged from the hospital. I was fine. I still had a bruise on my right forearm from the wreck, but I felt good. Saturday was going to be a fine weather day, and I let my friends know that I would be out on our local golf course in the morning. We had a wonderful time, but for me it was almost too emotional although I think I hid it well. This could have been the very last time I had fun playing golf with these guys. It's funny that the things that you do for entertainment aren't really that important in your life. You do these things when you have time, and they are not a high priority. But that day it felt like a stupid game of golf with these fine fellows was one of the most important things to do before I went in for brain surgery. All weekend I visited and talked with friends.

I never mentioned it before, but I am a Mass-going Catholic, and Pam and I are involved with the Church. Our priest heard my confession on Saturday and gave me anointing of the sick on Sunday. I thought if I were to die, right now would be the time to do it. I was ready and wasn't scared anymore about how anything was going to turn out.

I even went to work on Monday and Tuesday. My coworkers were full of questions and well wishes. Of course we kept things light and pestered each other like we usually do every day. I was starting to feel it all again that this might be my last time here. Pam had researched a book and had read excerpts from it to me, and it didn't scare me at the time but was starting to now. I do not remember the book, but this was a cancer survivor, and he had all kinds of ailments left over from his surgery. My surgeon said it was going to be like taking old gum off the bark of a tree but trying not to remove any of the bark. Plus, this tumor, if cancerous, would try to get into my spinal cord fluids and spread like wildfire through my body. At some point I asked my surgeon, "When I wake up and recover in a couple weeks or even a couple months, what can I expect to lose from this?"

She said that if I were a concert pianist, then I should worry about not being able to do that anymore.

I said, "Oh crap," and looked despondent.

She asked, "What?" I joked with her that I was a concert violinist. Her jaw dropped, but not for long—I let her in on the joke. I was glad for her confidence. Mike Tyson has been quoted as saying, "They're all tough until they get punched in the mouth." I was punched in the mouth.

On Tuesday afternoon I was on the verge of tears most of the day. It was another beautiful weather day, and I thought I may slip out and go to the golf course one last time after I went Saturday one last time. I didn't really care about the game; I just didn't want to be around work with my closest friends and the possibility of seeing me fall apart. That was the last thing I wanted them to see from me. I was scheduled to have a meeting with our director about some kind of safety concerns that afternoon, and I felt bad about skipping out on it, but I told my supervisor, who is a good friend of mine, that I was leaving early. I had enough composure to explain that leaving and walking out with my guys that day would be exceedingly difficult, and I didn't want to do it.

I really wasn't scared of dying, but coming out of the surgery unable to do the things I like to do, like golf, work, and provide for my family did scare me. The surgeon and her staff explained it all very well, and there were risks, huge risks, which could very well change my way of life. I really did not want any part of it.

So, like a coward, I left without giving a proper good-bye to everyone. I went to the course and played a little with my friends there but wished the whole time I would have stayed at work. My mind was messed up again.

That night I had my usual hour at the prayer chapel. We have a chapel where someone comes in at the top of the hour and replaces the one who is in there. We spend time with our Lord there. It is very peaceful, and this day I was particularly interested to go. I needed this. I came in and was all alone when, after a few minutes, the door opened, and my good friend and golfing buddy Garold came walking in and knelt down and prayed. Pretty soon in one- or two-minute intervals, Pete, Gilbert, and Joe, all good friends, came and prayed. I was happy to see them, but this was my hour and not theirs. They got up after a few minutes and came over and each placed a hand on my shoulders and prayed over me. They gave me their well wishes, and all of them left me alone to pray alone again. I left, and I was mentally prepared now.

Pam and I arrived at seven in the morning. I have been through several surgeries before, and time usually stood still waiting for things to happen. Not this time, however. Things went quickly. They had me back in a room with a wallpaper border of presents and stuffed bears. That was good for a little comedy relief with the nurse putting in IVs. I was visited by the anesthesiologist and by my surgeon. I was wheeled out and said my goodbye to Pam. I was out on the way down the hallway soon after saying goodbye. They didn't even let me know that I was on anything so I could say one last prayer. I was out before I arrived in the OR. That's OK. God knew how I felt.

I woke up from the surgery. It was like I was awake instantly because things were so strange. Pam was there to welcome me back, but I saw two of her, and both were standing on the wall. I laid on my back looking all around. The right wall had an air vent on it. I thought, "How strange." I also noticed that I felt my bed was turned over to the right side, and I should have fallen right out of it but didn't. The ceiling had a window. I soon realized that everything had shifted to the right. I dozed off again and woke up again later, and everything was back to where it was supposed to be. Maybe I was dreaming the room was on a right-handed axis before. I was not dreaming about the two of everything, however. It was October 7, and I would see double until the Friday after Thanksgiving. Getting back to the seventh, I remember thinking to myself, "When I wake up, check my fingers." On both hands I touched my thumbs to all my fingertips one at a time down from my index to my pinky finger and back up. *Wooohooo*! I still had my finger dexterity, and if I could do that then I could do anything in time.

My head and neck hurt badly, and I was on pain meds, so the whole parade of medical people coming in and talking to me was a blur. I can repeat it only because

Pam can recount it. This is during the peak time of COVID as well, so everyone was wearing a mask, which made it hard to distinguish who was who. I remember hearing that the surgeon thought she removed all of it. It took seven hours, but it was gone. The tumor was packed up and sent to the Mayo Clinic to see if it was malignant or not. The next few days in ICU would turn out to be the longest days of my life. I couldn't sleep very well, just an hour or two at a time. My head was swollen, and lying flat on my back had me lying on my sixteen stiches. I had double vision. A speech therapist came in and took me for a swallow test, and I don't remember it at all, but I guess I failed, and they put a feeding tube down my nose for about eight days or so. I also felt like I had a very tight belt or rubber band around my waist, which was extremely uncomfortable even though nothing was there. My feet tingled like they were being bitten by ants. After a week I finally got out of the intensive care unit and up to the tenth floor, which was called the penthouse. I awaited my results from the Mayo Clinic.

After I got up to the penthouse, I was able to get up to walk a little with a walker and a nurse or therapist to hold onto me. I really felt myself getting stronger. I still had this sinking feeling of "poor me" occasionally, but I was determined that I would get better and back to normal. The end was not in sight yet, but I knew it was there. It seemed like every morning when I woke up my daughter Jenn was there, sitting in a chair in the dark by the window. She came to visit after she got off work and stayed until Pam came from home. That was nice of her to stay with me, and after my feeding tube came out, she watched me eat breakfast. I even remember lightly tossing a squeeze toy back and forth with her. I felt like my voice was unintelligible, because if I listened to myself, I couldn't even tell what I was saying, so I stayed pretty quiet most of the time. I read a joke on Facebook and thought it was pretty funny, so I told it to Pam, and she recorded it with her phone and sent the video to family and friends. I watched it and wondered if anyone could understand, but for the first time in my life, watching my mannerisms and listening to my voice, I thought I really resembled my dad. I don't remember when exactly, but my results finally came back from Mayo: malignant. I had another hurdle to clear.

My walking was getting better and better, and I was walking that entire wing of the penthouse. I remember going around the south side of the wing and looking out of one of the windows. I would spy on a BBQ place, and it made me hungry for BBQ. But I was on a mission. I was determined to get better faster than anyone and go home. Pam and I passed the time by playing cards, and I thought I played well enough to prove my brain still functioned the same as before. One game Pam made a little mistake, which I saw, so

I immediately thought she was evaluating me. I told her to quit patronizing me. She assured me she wasn't, but she was happy that I was so alert and could catch something like that even if it was unintentional. The speech and physical therapist came and went for a week, and I finally got rid of that pestering feeding tube the next week on a Thursday, a week and a day later. I also remember that I took another swallow test. When I was loading up to go take it, a physical therapist showed up, and we couldn't get our workout that day.

Friday I was scheduled to go to a therapy hospital, but due to an insurance problem and being given too much blood pressure meds on that morning, I had to stay the weekend. My blood pressure went down to the sixties over forties. I was in no pain, but I was very weak. Boy did Pam ever let them have it for that one, and I was thinking, "*You go girl*!!!" but could not say anything. Up until that mishap, everything was great with the staff and hospital. A doctor on call had decided to get cute and prescribe me three times the amount of BP meds I was taking. Why? He thought my pressure was a bit high—who knows? Another day went by without physical therapy. Saturday and Sunday were uneventful, but PT doesn't work on weekends and the nursing staff was understaffed in the penthouse, so trying to get someone to accompany me on a walk of the hallways was nearly impossible. They put a belt around your chest, and someone held onto it and pulled you back straight if you were to go sideways. A nurse said on Sunday that she would find the time, but she never did. They had an aid who looked like she had just accepted the job right out of high school, and she said she would take me, but I didn't have a lot of confidence that she knew what to do. I didn't want to go, but Pam insisted, and Pam would go as well, so I relented and took a walk with the kid. I discovered that, after all the difficulties I had I had gone backward since last Wednesday. Walking was terribly difficult, and I was shakier than usual. I was still determined to leave.

Monday came, and I finally left Wesley at one in the afternoon. Except for the BP mishap, Wesley did an excellent job with me, and I couldn't have been more delighted with my surgeon. The nurses were skillful and very professional. Overall, under the circumstances it was a broad experience. I went to a therapy hospital, Saint Theresa's, on the northwest side of Wichita on Monday afternoon and met with some of the staff. They had me strapped into a wheelchair, and if I unbuckled my seat belt, an alarm would go off on the whole floor, and the staff on duty would come running. Pam and I found this out the hard way. I had to call a nurse every time I needed to go to the bathroom or get into bed. But just between you and me, I learned that the staff pushes some kind of button or buttons to turn off the alarm on the back of the chair. I took my cell phone, held it behind me and the back of the chair as best I could, and took a picture of the control box. I then could see where the disable button was on the box, and I could then reach around, disable the alarm, and go to the bathroom by myself. Shhh…don't tell anyone. I still needed to use a walker to go to the bathroom or to get anywhere. I suppose I was stupid, but there were people in that hospital that really needed help. They were in seemingly much worse shape than I. They were mostly heart attack and stroke victims. By the looks of it, I was the youngest person there at the grand old age of fifty-six. I always wondered though that the staff didn't pay much attention to rule breakers, because otherwise someone would question how I got into bed or if I ever went to the bathroom.

The day I arrived, Monday, someone came in that evening and wrote my Tuesday schedule on a white-board on the wall. The day was full of activity. I was determined to get out of this hospital as fast as possible, so I would do everything asked of me and more. Drill Sergeant Jones taught me well. We decided it was time for Pam to go back to work now, because my schedule was full of activities, but she would come back a couple of evenings.

That next morning I began my physical, occupa-tional, and speech therapy. I have to say, I'm not too big on someone I don't know being in the shower room with me, but I got cleaned up and shaved during occupational therapy. I did appreciate the help and the little helpful tidbits she gave me for when I got to go home. I was still eating thickened food at this point, water thicker than molasses. Have you ever eaten coffee with a spoon? The speech therapist here worked with me and gave me all kinds of exercises to do during the day to get my swallow muscles back in shape. Physical therapy was the big one. I felt I had to work this one the hardest of all to get into shape and be allowed to go home. I was determined. I would walk down the hallway, and, if asked if I wanted to take a break and sit for a while, I said, "Nope. Let's go!" It's the same thing with going up and down stairs. I did everything I was asked to do and more. I worked to the point of sweating and panting.

The hardest though, was balancing on all the little steppers they have that sway you back and forth. One day the PT had me walking without a walker, and he was not holding onto me, and I was walking down the hallway bouncing a blue racquetball back and forth from my left hand to my right and back again. It worked well if I bounced it the same way every time, but once I bounced it out too far in front of me, and I reached for it with my right hand, lost my balance, slammed right into the wall on the right, and I hit the floor. Here came the chest belt again.

For some reason my sweet tooth was highly active, but sugar was not a friend to my stomach. It didn't matter too much, as I rarely got anything sweet besides maybe pudding anyway due to my diet of thickened liquids. One day my therapist was walking me to the room where we practiced going up and down stairs and other obstacles. She had a belt around me while I was scooting along with my walker. We had to go down another wing, and it had a nurse's station at the front. On the counter was a plastic jack-o'-lantern loaded to the top with fun-size chocolate bars. I had to get me one of those pieces of candy! But how? I was busy going up and down stairs and hatching a plan. Now I must stop here to say that fun-size pieces are no fun. I call them piss-me-off size—they're just small enough to piss me off that I don't have more. Back to the story. After another grueling sweaty therapy session, I made sure that I was on the left side and my therapist was on my right. We left the room and meandered down the hallways back to my room. I don't remember the conversation, but I had decided that I would regale her with stories of yore and get her to laughing and having a good time. She held on, of course, but she was at a constant giggle when we walked by that jack-o'-lantern. Here was my chance! As I sauntered by, I let go of my walker with my left hand and as fast as I could, I reached up and grabbed a Kit Kat and slipped in into my pants pocket without missing a step. I was as fast as lightning, and she never noticed a thing. I went back to my room and slowly devoured this little morsel of pure happiness, even though it tasted different to me at the time.

They encouraged me to exercise on my own as much as I wanted, but my exercise on my own consisted of sitting in my wheelchair and using my feet to pitter patter my way around the hallways in a circle. I tried to stay out of the way of the other patients who during the day would go up and down to their own therapy sessions.

One day I was going to a session of my own, and we went to the west end of the hallway with a nurse's station and a little break area consisting of table and chairs for folks to have lunch or for patients to sit and visit with multiple visitors at once, even though that sort of thing wasn't allowed during these COVID times. My therapist and I passed by this break area one day, and it was filled with the fixings for a party: cake, cookies, and all sorts of goodies. My mind started to race about how I could swipe one of those cookies. I couldn't get close enough to the table to swipe away a cookie like I had the little fun-size Kit Kat; I had to devise a plan.

We finished my therapy, and we always went around the long way of the wing back to our rooms. It just gave us a bit more exercise, but that long way was not going by the goodies. Rats! Foiled again! I got my seatbelt put on in my wheelchair once I got back to my room. Now was my chance to go on recon and produce a plan to get a cookie. I didn't care if anyone else was going up and down the hallway. These people were in the way of my mission, and someone might get hurt in the process. "Collateral damage," I thought. "These people are expendable as far as my hunger and cookies are concerned." I got out in the hallway and stayed close to the wall.

The nurse's station was tall, and I thought I could quietly slip by anyone who was there, as my head was lower than the height of the station. I was lucky! No one was there! I saw my chance, like I had crossed the road during war games. I made my move, and my feet moved faster than a speeding Fred Flintstone car as I rounded the desk. Fortune smiles on the bold! I could taste one of those big cookies now! The break room came into sight and, like a magician, poof! All the goodies had disappeared, and there wasn't even a clue that a party had even been had. I was disappointed to say the least. But I did have Pam. One of those evenings, she snuck in a little carton of ice cream in her purse. She is such an outlaw rule breaker.

I think it was Tuesday night, and they moved a new neighbor into the room next to mine. Until it was time for sleeping, all the doors to every room were left open. Now I do feel sorry for anybody who has been admitted to any kind of hospital; I wish them all well. But this lady felt compelled to call half of Wichita, Kansas to tell them about the stroke she had and then the other half of Wichita would call her. She had a ringtone that was the beginning notes of "My Heart Will Go On" by Celine Dion. You know the song from the movie *Titanic*? I must have heard her phone ring about a hundred times that night and more the following days. I called her Rose after the movie character. I thought about hollering, "Rose, I'm going to come beat the crap out of Jack unless you turn that damn ringtone down," but I didn't. I used to like that song, but every time I hear the opening notes even to this day, it reminds me of Rose next door in the therapy hospital.

I worked hard and kept a cheerful outlook with everyone I worked with. It worked; I stayed less than a week, and they let me go on that Friday. The original thought was that I was going to be there two or three weeks.

The main reason they let me go so early, though, was because my house is set up well for someone like me: a walk-in shower, no stairs to speak of, except for the basement stairs, and I don't have to go up and down them right now. My daughter Melanie was coming to stay for a while with the kids and stay with me during the day while Pam worked. That was really what made their decision easy—someone was going to be home with me during the day, so they cut me loose. The staff were very professional and knowledgeable.

I suppose it's the kid in me or the soldier in me, but I always like to hear the therapists tell me what a good patient I am. I heard it more than once and in three different therapy departments that working with me is a delight. Most patients need their teeth pulled to get them to take a step, and I had seen that fact with my own eyes as these folks could barely make it down the hallway, but I was eager for every step. I remember the two main physical therapists I worked with at St. Theresa's said that if every patient had my drive, then their job would be much easier. Yes, I like to hear that, but I just wanted to get better quicker. Now that I was going home that sort of thing didn't stop. As it turned out, I was only getting started.

As I sat on my bed waiting for my discharge, I read an article written by a girl who had tried every Dairy Queen Blizzard and ranked them in order from worst to best. I read her complaints about the kinds on the lower end of the rankings, and she said right away that something has to be last even if it's good. It was all based on her personal preference, but she said her favorite was the New York cheesecake with strawberry. I told Pam that on the way home we had to stop at Dairy Queen in Goddard and get a Blizzard. I ordered the New York cheesecake with strawberries. It was delicious. We even took a picture of me with my eyepatch scooping ice cream and posted it on Facebook. On the drive home I was seeing more than double. The farther away I looked down the road, the more roads I saw. Between the road we were on and the two lanes coming back the other way, it looked like the mix master in Dallas. I either closed my eyes or put my eye patch back on.

Melanie, my son-in-law Dan, and my two grand-daughters at the time, Coraline, age two and a half, and Bridget, four months, came for a visit the weekend I got home. Melanie and the kids were going to stay for a while and Dan, who is a teacher, was going to go back home and continue teaching. Mel, as she is affection-ately nicknamed, made life easier for both Pam and me. She cooked and cleaned, did laundry, and most importantly got me to physical and speech therapy at our local hospital and gave me rides to radiation for a week when it first started. The kids kept me busy play-ing, eating, and reading books. I told folks that I had a B and B, but it stood for books and bottles instead of bed and breakfast. The most important thing Mel did was to keep me exercising. We would pack up the kids and load Bridget up in a stroller and Coraline would either ride along or walk, but we would hit the streets to get some exercise. I'm sure we looked strange walking down the road with a lady pushing a baby stroller and an old man barely creeping along with a walker. It could be chilly some days, but we bundled up when we had to and kept going. At first we went up and down our street. After a couple times of that, we went around the block, and it wasn't long before I had the strength to go four or five blocks south, turn right for a block, and then come back. Then we walked north of the house a block or two and then would go four to five south. In my walks with the kids, I saw a few friends and people I knew drive by and stare at us. Like I said, I'm sure we looked funny, but once again I was determined, but on days when I lacked the drive, Mel provided it for me. Both my kids were an immense help in getting me through all this.

I had to go to another hospital, St. Francis, to get a spinal tap. I always thought that it was just a movie. The spinal tap took a sample of my cerebral spinal fluid to see if the tumor had shed any malignant cells into my spinal column, where they could spread to other places in my body. Looking at my initial MRI, I could see where it was attached to my spinal cord; it was causing a bend in it trying to get in to travel down the spinal fluid highway.

A few days later, I had to go to Wesley hospital and talk to the oncologist there about starting radiation. He filled Pam and me in on what was going to happen and what to expect. As he talked to me, I still had this thought that it's just another thing I had to do. Attack it hard, do what you are told, and it'll soon all be over. At the end of the consult, however, he let us have the good news that the results of the spinal tap were in, and the tumor did *not* infiltrate my cerebrospinal fluid. I remember tapping the table like playing a drum. I finally received some good news, a battle I didn't have to fight. I tell people all the time that when I got that news, I thanked God again and, on the inside, I felt like a hundred little kids waking up on Christmas morning.

I started physical therapy in my hometown hospital, and my therapist, Megan, who is a friend of mine through church, really worked hard with me and for me. I treated her plan very much like the plans I had at the therapy hospital, but without any jack-o'-lanterns. Do more than what I was asked and never take a break. Every day I came in and rode a stationary bike to get warmed up first. Each day I made it a point to go farther than the time before, even when the difficulty of the bike pedal tension had been adjusted up. We went for walks down the hallway while looking extremely up or extremely down and side to side. I did an old football drill of walking sideways and brought my legs over in front and back of each other. I called this dancing down the hallway and would sing a song while doing it. Might as well have fun, plus it made Megan laugh. I did other exercises as well, like standing and trying to balance on a rocking board, standing on one foot, too many things to remember now. I graduated to doing these exercises while throwing a ball back and forth with her. She always found it remarkable that I could do the exercises better if there was ball tossing involved. I told her it's my competitive nature kicking in while playing ball. Other than that, I just like to play with my balls. That brought howls of laughter from the whole staff.

Megan really helped me and every day gave me increased courage to do things on my own. One of the things we did was walk on a raised padded bar, about an inch high and four or five inches wide. I would walk forward on it, heel to toe, backward, and sometimes I would turn around on it and walk forward the other way. I was getting good at this exercise, still not good enough to pass a law enforcement officer's sobriety test, but better. One day I asked her to do this without a belt around my waist for her to hold onto. I wanted to fly solo. She didn't think it was a good idea, but if you've read this far, you know by now that I never take no for an answer when I really want something. I pestered her about it until she relented. I don't remember, but this could have taken more than one or two visits to convince her, but on this day, after my prodding, she was finally going to let me go solo.

Their little space in our local hospital was crowded with all kinds of tools to use for all kinds of different therapies. They didn't have nearly enough space to work with patients, much less room for all their equipment. They did the best they could with the space they had and put things on the wall or leaned up against the walls, in office spaces, every nook and cranny. She laid these things on the floor and one end was close to the south wall, the end where I turn around or go backward. There was one of those small trampolines leaning up against the wall there. I walked down the bar just fine and when I got to the end, I went to turn around. I don't know how she could control me so well with that belt when

I had it on, but without it she was nearly helpless trying to control me. As I turned, I fell off the bar and started to fall backward. Luckily for me that trampoline was there, and I hit it with my ass just right and was able to bounce right back up.

I wish it were so simple. As I was falling, I was flailing my arms, and I wound up knocking some things down that were next to the trampoline and making a lot of noise. The whole staff came running into the little room we were in. We both stood there acting as if nothing happened, but the things spread about on the floor told a different story. Megan had a look on her face like, "Oh hell, here it comes." I felt terrible. It was my entire fault. I tried talking her into it and would not shut up about it over at least a couple days of pestering until I got my way. We admitted that a little fall had happened. I explained to her manager that it was all my fault, I was convinced I could do this without assistance, had already done it without assistance many times even though the belt was on me, but I kept asking and pestering. It was a challenge and I had to face it sometime, so it might as well be here. I went several more times, but I let my therapist decide on what and how we would do anything. No more suggestions from me. Megan is an excellent physical therapist, a friend in fact, and I didn't want to risk getting her in trouble. Truth be known, the whole staff knew what kind of pain I could be.

After I was done sweating through physical therapy, I went down the hallway to speech therapy. It was less taxing on the body, but I spent thirty minutes to an hour doing mouth and throat exercises. For a couple weeks after getting home, I was still on a thickened liquid diet, and I hated it and was determined to get over that as fast as possible as well. Both of my therapists did an excellent job with me, and I give them a lot of the credit for helping me get over a few humps much faster than usual. I think both could clearly see that I have extraordinarily little patience for not making progress.

After a while I started radiation at Wesley in Wichita. Every day, Monday through Friday, we went to Wichita. Mel drove at first, but after five weeks of staying with me, it was time to go home. Dan came back and stayed for Thanksgiving and then hauled his little family back home. I missed Mel and the little ones terribly. I thank God for them every day for the help they gave me during this time. Pam started driving me. The actual treatment didn't take but seven minutes by my account. They made a mask that fit exactly over my face, and they strapped it down with my head underneath it to a table. The mask was meant to hold me perfectly still. After a couple of weeks, I thought I could drive, but I had to prove it to Pam. There are no trampolines to pick you up on the highway. Once I proved I could drive, Pam could stay at work, and I drove myself. I finally got clearance to go back to work on December

14 with a few work restrictions—a bit early, but I was eager to get started. I knew that my crew would take care of me and make sure that I didn't screw myself or a machine up, and my buddy Mike in particular would keep an eye on me. But by one in the afternoon, I was beat. I was completely worn out. After work ended at two thirty, I went to Wesley for radiation treatment. For some reason after lying on that table for a few minutes, getting up and walking was getting difficult. I think I was still having trouble with blood pressure rising and falling with lying down and standing. After a minute I was fine and jumped in the car and went home. I had eleven days off from work during what is called Christman shutdown. My friends had to work but I wasn't allowed, as most projects are very physical and the project schedule had already been completed. I didn't mind being left out. I knew I came back to work a little early and should have probably stayed out until January anyway. This eleven-day break would definitely help.

I went back in January, and a few of my symptoms remained. I still felt like I had a belt just below my chest, and it was very tight. My left hand got to feeling much better, but my right hand was still numb but useful to a point. My skull was numb to the touch on my right side. That didn't bother my work except that my hair itched. At times it felt like an ice pick was trying to get out of my head for a couple of seconds. I wasn't myself yet, but I was determined to go and make a good hand.

I quickly found out that I had lost some short-term memory. There were people who had worked there for years that I recognized but didn't know their names.

On a website dedicated to people who have or have had an ependymoma, I have read many testimonies of what folks have gone through. I felt sorry for these people because they had to wait until they were symptomatic for their tumors to be found. Most of these people were worse off than I was. I could imagine having things like paralyzed feet, legs, or arms. At this point in writing, it's been almost five months already, and all I have left is the ice pick in my head, my right hand is still numb, and I have a rubber band around me just below my chest that is sometimes very tight and sometimes not so much. I get tired easily, and as someone explained in one of the testimonies I read, your energy is a candy dish, and when the candy is gone for the day, it doesn't fill back up until you get a good night's rest. My wife showed me another article that talks about the spoon theory, which is the same concept except with spoons.

I was a complete ass, and an uneducated one at that. I always wondered why there is so much fuss about cancer. Our small town has had these overnight walks with teams that represent cancer survivors, and I thought, "Why? Yes, having cancer is terrible, but you have it, it is gone, and you go on with the rest of your life." It took me getting it to realize that even when you do not have it anymore, you're never ever really rid of it. The feeling it leaves you with is more than what a broken arm or a replaced knee, a fused back or even a common cold will leave you with. It is hard to describe, but it's like the way you feel violated when someone breaks into your house and ransacks the place and steals your stuff. Cancer violates your body, and you do not forget it. The initial worry and fear, the unknown, then the surgery, the many symptoms that you have are all new to a person, me included. The work you put in trying to get back in your body what you lost, and it's a long time coming. The constant thought of "What happens if it comes back?" Hey, I have always considered myself a tough guy, mentally and physically, but this stuff tests you. Therapists, your spouse, your kids, and other family and relatives will tell you that you did great. They're happy how progress is going, they're proud of you, and you hear it but don't let it sink in because it may not be over yet. All cancer survivors do it, and I do it too. I go every three months for a brain and spinal MRI and an oncology consult after the MRI gets read. I'm always thinking I have three months, then the worry starts to sink in again. It never really leaves. They have these walks and other programs to raise awareness. I thought I was aware, but I was wrong. I was never aware until it hit me personally.

This book could have been how God has been watching over me. Who knows? That may be my next book. It gives me great peace to know that God loves me. I feel he has a plan for me that I must fulfill; that's why I had the experience I had with the car accident and the early finding. God does watch over me and has shown me many miracles past any normal explanation. Those are for my next book, because he left me with a book's worth of writing to tell you his success stories in my life.

As I come back to writing, I am now three years from my surgery. I have had eating complications for a long time; swallowing is not always a given. I can have a mouthful of food, and it just sits in the back of my throat wondering what to do. I am sure it is weird to be an ordinary person to try to imagine what it's like to forget how to swallow, but my muscles just forget. I can see that I forget lots of things. Pam tells me that we are going to do something tomorrow, and when tomorrow comes, I have forgotten she ever told me. I've always been bad with names, but I'm especially bad now. My buddy at work Mike always has to remind me of people's names. I think he is pretty good at keeping secrets, because I seem to hide my forgetfulness well. My balance is still not what it used to be either. I sway all the time unless I can ground myself by pushing my leg or arm up against something to give me an anchor. I get up from a chair and get the lean going forward and take a couple extras steps. Just little things really. These problems have become normal for me now. They have been with me for so long I don't recognize them as problems anymore. At first in the early days, I always told Pam that if this thing ever comes back, I'm just going to slide out slowly. I don't have the strength or the desire to fight it. Now three years later and three granddaughters and one grandson on the way, I've changed my mind. If round two ever happens, I'm ready to punch this sucker out again.

I call this part of the book, this chapter, an unwanted visitor. Sure, this time of my life can be considered bad, but so much good has come from it. Friends have proven to be friends; my children have helped more than I can ever repay. Chili, cookies, and many more meals were delivered with love to us when I got home. I appreciated it and somehow remember it all. But there was one constant, one person who I couldn't see me doing anything without, and that's my wife, Pam. She has been everything for me. When my spirits were up, she was my cheerleader. When I was down, she was my therapist and still my cheerleader. She was my everything. I often see and hear from people who have nobody like I do in their life, and I often have wondered how they manage. I couldn't manage at all if it weren't for Pam, and I'm not just talking about this chapter about cancer. Pam 'n' Felix, Felix 'n' Pam. Somehow we just go together. We don't always agree on everything, but we make it work. She is the one love of my life, my rock that keeps me steady, and the rock I'll never throw away.

TIME MOVES ON

PAM TO THE RESCUE

Our kids are gone to live their own lives now, so that leaves Pam and me to an empty nest. We travel to see our grandkids every chance we get, but we have also started to take little weekend excursions to not-very-far-away places. Mostly we like to go hiking around lakes, hills, and such. One weekend we went to Palo Duro Canyon. We went in August, the hottest part of the year. It was an extremely sweltering day, well over a hundred degrees during the afternoons. We did our research on all the hiking trails and decided to go on the longest one, a more than three-mile trek up and down through a canyon that ends with twin buttes that have been used in many western films. The park rangers were out in full force that day, and signs were all over that said to take a gallon of water per person on any hike that day due to the heat. We took several bottles of water in a cheap little cloth cooler. We did not take quite the suggested gallon per person, but we had a gallon and a half, plus we thought we would drink plenty of water right before we took off.

The trails at Palo Duro are marked every tenth of a mile. It was a nice trek with plenty of views of the desert and hills, and not too many people were out even for a Saturday. We did run across a bicyclist going out and then coming back. We crossed paths with a couple, a little younger than us, coming back from the end of the trail. The wife looked pretty worn out to me as we passed and said our hellos. Pam decided to stop at the three-mile marker, stating that she had to get back yet and had better stop. I went forward to see the buttes, about another three tenths of a mile. I made my way back to where Pam had stopped. The park was nice enough to put benches with covers over the top of them to block the sun in spots along the trail. We stopped at a couple on the way back and had a sip of water. The trail was up and down but did not have any steps to speak of. We got to the top of this one hill, miles away from the trailhead, and this couple that we had passed earlier while they were on the way back was sitting on this bench under a sun shelter. I was right; this lady looked awful. The husband thought she would be OK in a little while and could continue once the sun went behind a cloud. Yeah, whatever, this gal was going to die out here if she tried to go on. We still had two bottles of water left and Pam, being a medical assistant, had her lie down and sip some of our water because they had been out for a while now. We all had our phones but did not have any service out there. We all thought it best if someone went for help. I thought Pam needed to stay with her in case things got worse. The husband should not leave his wife, so that left me. I wondered where that bicyclist was when I needed him.

I took off jogging downhill. I am in no way in shape to do this, but it had to be done. When I started to go uphill, I walked and caught my breath, but when going downhill, I let my inertia guide me down. It was only 1.2 miles, but I wasn't in army shape or age, and I left our water with Pam to give to the poor gal. I stayed after it and finally got down to the trailhead. A four-wheeler was just leaving headed up the trail. I stopped the two rangers on it and told them that a lady was having heat exhaustion or a stroke at the 1.2-mile shelter. They said they knew because they had just gotten a call. Well crap! What did I just run through this burning canyon for? And why didn't I try to call 911 at some point in my journey? I wasn't thinking; I was just bearing down on getting down to the trailhead as fast as I could without heat exhaustion bearing down on me as well.

I went to our car and opened the trunk to a big cooler full of iced-down bottles of water. I opened a bottle and sat down in the trunk, leaning on the cooler with my legs hanging out on the outside looking like a real hillbilly. I didn't care; I was spent. I was far from done though. Pam was still up the trail without water. I drank another bottle quickly, filled my shorts pockets with three or four bottles of water, and headed back up the trail. I didn't run—I probably couldn't. Soon the four-wheeler was coming down with the lady lying on a gurney and her husband kind of hanging onto the side. She still looked in bad shape to me, and the husband gave a wave as they went by. I kept going. Pam couldn't catch a ride, so she was on foot. I only hoped that the rangers gave her some water. I was at the bottom of a big, steep hill, getting myself ready to dig in to muster up the strength to go up, when I heard my name called. I looked up, and it was Pam at the top of the hill waving at me. I had not been so delighted and excited to see her in a long time. I gave her a bottle of water, and she drank it slowly as I turned around at the 0.6-mile marker. I had made it halfway back.

Pam is the hero of this story. She kept that gal comfortable, fanned her, administered slowly to her all our water, and talked to her to keep her going. Pam also finally got enough phone signal to make a call.

I found out later that when the rangers got there, they asked how she was doing. The lady said, "I'll be OK as long as I have Pam with me." Funny—I feel the same way.

We slowly walked back and met a family with small kids coming up the trail. They asked if it was still a long way from the end, and we said yes, and if you didn't bring enough water, you had better turn back. The rangers had already taken one lady down from the trail today. The dad said there was an ambulance at the trailhead, and he had wondered why. He and his family turned around because they only had one gallon of water for a family of four or five, I don't remember. Wise choice.

We got down to the trailhead, drank some more water, and left. We made our way out of the canyon and back into Amarillo. I was done in. I managed to eat a steak and spray paint "FLEX" on a Cadillac at the Cadillac ranch. I'd like to go back someday, but maybe in April or November.

FORE!

Where we really love to travel to is Wisconsin to visit our grandchildren. Oh, we like to visit our daughter and son-in-law too. In the summer my son-in-law Dan and I like to go golfing on their little nine-hole golf course just outside of town. It's a nice, hilly course. We were on the sixth hole one day when we came up behind a foursome of slow-playing ladies. They weren't as much slow as they were bad. We finally got to hole number nine, which is a par five. We were right on their tails, so we had to wait to tee off. After they had moved along, I hit a nice drive right down the middle. Dan had a longer drive but over on the right side in the rough. We drove up to my ball. We waited on these ladies again, and they finally moved along after their fourth or fifth shot. I decided to hit my ball while I was still young. I addressed the ball, took a smooth swing, and *boom*!!!! It took off like a rocket. I caught it pure like you're supposed to. It sailed like it was on the wings of an angel, and it was heading right at where those ladies were standing. It hit the ground and rolled right on by them and their carts. They turned around, and all I heard was muffled sounds like Charlie Brown's teacher. We went to find Dan's ball in the rough but to also hide in the tall grass. Dan can consistently hit his ball farther than me, so we decided to wait this time. The ladies moved up on the green and eventually putted out and left for the clubhouse. We chipped on and putted out.

We were going to start the back nine, and Dan asked if I wanted a Gatorade. I said, "Yes, but I am not going in that clubhouse and getting into a fight with four women." We drove around to hole one, and Dan went inside to get a couple of bottles of Gatorade. The clubhouse has a nice balcony for people to sit on facing the number one tee box. A lady came walking out on that balcony, leaned over with her forearms on the rail and went on a tirade. She said something to the effect that everyone has to wait out here, and it won't do me any good to be in a rush, yada, yada, yada. She finally decided to take a breath, so that allowed me to retort. I told her I was sorry; I didn't think I could hit a ball that far, and that was one of the best, longest, purest three woods I have ever hit in my life. "From where you turned around and saw me, weren't you impressed?" She stood leaning on that railing and just shook her head no. I was hoping to get a laugh or at least a smile, but alas, no. "Come on Dan, hurry up with that Gatorade!" Dan finally came down with the drinks. Sometimes when I think back like right now as I write, I wonder if he went in there and pointed me out sitting in that cart at hole number one. Hmmm…

MY SARCASM TEAM HAS A GOLFING PROBLEM

Through the years I played a lot of softball, but when I got too seasoned for that, I started to play golf. I play at our local country club, and I'll play with anyone, but I usually play with my boys, my group. My group consists of two guys in their eighties and a sample of sixty- and seventy-year-old guys. It's just pure fun not only to play golf with these guys, but to listen to what they have to say. We have two Bobs, and they are in their eighties. One we call Mr. Automatic because he rarely misses the fairway but always complains how he didn't hit it long enough. He'd hit one down the middle and one of us would say, "Wow, look at that!" He'd say sarcastically, "Yeah, you look at it." Bob, our other senior member, is the best golfer of the group. When he was in his seventies and now in his eighties, he would often shoot under his age. The rest of us never say as much, but we cherish this time we have with these fine gentlemen.

We gamble a quarter playing a skins game. A skins game is where everybody plays their own ball to the hole. If one person has a lower score on that hole than everyone else, he wins a quarter from everyone. If two or more tie, then that quarter goes onto the next hole, and it is worth two quarters a person and so on. The person who won the last "skin" always has the honor of hitting off the tee box first. The one with the worst score hits last, or "from the back of the bus." When you play five guys, though, it can get confusing who hits when.

Years ago we had a guy out there, Dennis, who was quite the character. Dennis was left-handed like me. In those days, the Bobs were in their sixties, and it wasn't unusual to play forty holes or more a day even on the hottest of days. I worked at night and would join them in the afternoon. Dennis loved his Natural Light and would drink it the entire time he played. One Saturday we had a tournament at the club, and I invited Rick out to play in it. You remember Rick with the crash test dummy? Rick and I showed up and took off in my cart to go play a hole or two and get loosened up. We could see the parking lot from hole six, and I spotted Dennis sitting on his tailgate drinking a beer. It was about seven thirty in the morning, and introductions aside, I said, "Dennis, are you drinking already?"

Dennis said with a grin, "You can't drink all day unless you start first thing in the morning." Rick about lost it. It did seem like the more he drank the better he played.

There are a lot of sayings and catch phrases that have been invented over the years. One of our members, Garold, even went as far as to come up with a list of sayings, phrases, and excuses and numbered them. I don't have that list anymore, or it may even be some-where in my bag, and I don't remember the full list, but I do remember number one was !@#$%^%$$%^&!!! So now, with the aid of this list, the next time I'm on the number two tee box and I severely slice my ball into a wheat field across the road, all I have to do is simply scream, "Number one!!!!!"

All the numbers on Garold's list had an actual story behind them from our group. One day a guy showed up who often played with us when we didn't have four or five. He showed up later in the day and wouldn't play nearly as many holes as the rest of us. He was a very good golfer, but he used every excuse in the book when things didn't go his way. He even made up some that weren't in the book. One day he had a three-foot putt, and he carefully lined it up and missed. He muttered, "Fu$%^g greenskeeper!" He blamed missing a little putt on the greenskeeper. Bob let him have it for that. Bob didn't like his excuses most any day, but that day he had had it up to his eyeballs. The rest of us about died laughing at this guy. From that day forward, if anyone missed a little putt, the greenskeeper got an earful. It became number thirteen, I think.

One day we were on the tee box in a group of five. It's easy to forget who teed off and who didn't. One day Dennis was last, which is unusual. We all took our turns hitting our drivers, and we all walked off the tee box and toward our carts. Dennis was standing on the tee box staring at the rest of us, cleared his throat to get our attention and said, "What am I, chopped liver?" We all laughed, and each of us had a turn or two over the years to use it. It was number eight or something.

Another hazard of hitting five off a tee is that you can forget not only where you hit your ball, but also where everyone else hit theirs. One day Mark hit his ball and grounded it through the grass, and it came to stop about sixteen yards away. It was past the ladies' tee, so he didn't have to play the hole with his taiwhacker out. The rest of us teed off, and we all went to our own carts and took off. We usually took off like a bat out of hell, but Mark came to an almost dead stop at his ball, causing everyone else to slam on their brakes. Dennis hollered out, "What are we stopping here for?" Yeah, maybe it's not funny now but hit your tee shot about thirty yards, then drive off and stop to hit it. Around my guys you'll get a chorus of "Number six!"

Dennis didn't hit his drives very high or long in the air, but when they hit the ground, they would roll a good distance. He'd hit his ball and holler at the top of his lungs, "You gotta roll!" These days at my age, I do it too, but not as loud.

One day Dennis had to make a long ten-to-thirteen-foot putt downhill to win a long line of holes in our skins game, which would've put a huge dent in my change bag on my cart. I decided to try a little psychology and said to Dennis at this crucial time in his putt, "Dennis, I hope you're having fun and enjoying this beautiful weather. It really is nice out here with all of us together for a lively game of golf. For you, my friend, I want nothing more than for you to enjoy the day, enjoy your friends, have a good round, and have a good score. But mostly what I want you to do is to miss this putt." He laughed so hard he had to reset himself over the ball. Then he sank it.

A few times a year we play in tournaments on other courses. Usually it is Garold, Mark, me, and someone we pick up to play. A few times we've picked up Tyler. Now Tyler is not a golfer, and he would be the first one to tell you as much, but he is a great guy. He takes a lot of ribbing from us, and he gives a little back.

We have played in the Kansas Knights of Columbus golf tournament, which may sound like something special, but it is just another excuse to get together to hack at golf balls. We have to travel to play at these, so we usually carpool. It saves on gas, and I can be the designated driver for everyone else on the way home. One day in Topeka, I think, Mark, Garold, and I were in the parking lot, and Tyler came driving up. He came separately from us for some reason. He got out, and after pleasantries he opened his trunk to get his bag of clubs out and started to put on his golf shoes. The ride had been long, and he stretched out his legs and began to tie his shoes by propping his foot up on his open trunk. Tyler complained that his butt was hurting. I think Mark commented that maybe he and his wife were doing it wrong. How in the hell did he have all those kids anyway? Tyler currently has six children, and when you have kids as wonderful as his, why stop? `

We play four-man scrambles and always let Tyler putt first so if he misses it, the rest of us can read his and adjust. He lined up a ball one day, and the rest of us were behind him to watch his putt when he asked, "How do my feet look?" One of us told him something to the effect of "Well you have a corn on one foot and are flat footed on the other...What the hell does it matter what your feet look like?" Ever since then, about four times a round, when he lines up on a putt, we remind him not to worry, his feet look good.

Golf for us isn't a sport; it's what we do. It's like a party only with golf clubs and golf balls. I have really grown to cherish this time outside with all my friends. Mr. Automatic has passed on now, and I will miss him and miss playing golf with him.

BOARD OF DIRECTORS OR CAST OF CHARACTERS?

The years have passed, and I have stayed clean of any form of cancer, as I do get fresh pictures of my brain every six months whether I can afford them or not. In a couple of years, it'll be stretched out to yearly. It was early in my recovery period when I got a letter in the mail asking if I had any interest in joining the board of directors of our local nonprofit theatre. I thought Pam and I have spent enough money on tickets and popcorn over the years that we should own it by now, so why not? A member of the board of directors sounds so professional and businesslike. The cast of characters that make up this group of people aren't exactly your suit-wearing types, but I will say that a more caring group of people all joined together with one goal of keeping the old theater going for the community cannot be found.

COVID had taken its toll on all businesses, but any business whose main income came from people gathering indoors, particularly for entertainment, got hit harder than most. Technology presented streaming services to watch the latest movies, and TVs have gotten as big as the actual walls they hang from and more affordable too. By the time theaters started up again, the streaming services had such a firm grasp on the industry that some theaters didn't survive.

To raise funds to keep the doors open, we had to come up with ways to make money besides movies and asking for donations too many times. We decided to get clever and go a little further than most people would. Now here is where the colorful characters and funny stories begin.

Halloween

It was decided that we would turn the theatre into a haunted house, except it was a theatre. We would transform the lobby and two bathrooms into a haunted house, and as patrons made their way through, they eventually made their way into the auditorium where they would watch a scary movie. The catch was that while the movie was playing, our zany cast of crazies all dressed up as ghouls and ghosts would interact with the crowd.

Now I would be seriously remiss if I didn't add a little mention to "the ones who get it done." We always boast we are a team, and we are, but in our projects, there is a small group of core people who are always there planning, decorating, doing everything behind the scenes. Oh sure, you can walk into the lobby, buy a soda and a bag of popcorn, and walk through the black curtain only to be met by a clown or monster that chases you into the women's bathroom. But who hung that curtain? Who arranged getting it? It's the behind the scenes, showing up nightly after a full day of work somewhere else doing something else that gets forgotten, but I don't forget. Yes, it's a team thing, I suppose, but these folks, Deena, Angie, Belinda, Judy, and now Clyde, make it all go. And after the preliminary work, they partake in the character work, sell tickets, work concessions, and do the technical work, and when it's all over they tear it all down. The rest of us help where we can but these folks make it all go. These people never cease to amaze me. Judy is Deena and Angie's Mom. She works like three people. When I grow up, I want to be just like her.

We needed people to be scary monsters, and we had a selection of characters. Everyone took to this project well—some too well. Our first year we had Steve and Courtney to help us out, and Courtney is a makeup expert. They are known as Mr. and Mrs. Halloween, and the label was cemented by one of our local newscasters when doing a story on us. Next we have Paula, who is also a makeup expert in her own right and never ceases to amaze me with her creativity in almost anything, decorating, makeup, or acting. Her characters usually freak me out, and I'm dressed up as well. Amanda is an extremely talented artist and can build anything out of nearly anything. Plus she screams like a wild naked banshee.

I Ain't No Dummy

When decorating the theatre, I had the bright idea to tie a string from a speaker holder up on the balcony down to the handrail to the steps up to an emergency exit by the stage. My plan was to take this real ventriloquist dummy, hang him from a rope, and slide him down the string. I tested my idea, and it didn't work too well. The dummy weighed too much and caused the string to drag in the middle. I took the dummy off and put him in a seat on the balcony. I found a little witch that lit up that was much lighter. I had a new plan! I would throw the witch down the string, and when people would look up at the lit-up witch, which would take up their attention, then they could be scared out of their wits by our scarers on the floor sneaking up on them and giving them the proverbial boo! The witch would also only go about halfway down and get stuck. Ding! Another idea! I went home and got a trusty Zebco 33 rod and reel and tied onto the witch so when I threw her out, I could make her jump and reel back up. I left the whole thing hooked up and ready to go on the balcony.

The first night came, and we were all amped up. I was a bloody, ghostly rodeo clown. Mostly I wasn't scary as much as funny, I suppose, but I enjoyed myself, and others seemed to enjoy the act so what the heck. With the auditorium quiet, I went running down the south aisle, which, in my condition at the time, was a risky think to do, rapidly slapping my ass with my cowboy hat like I was urging on a racing steed across the prairie and whooping and hollering like a ghoulish cowboy. I rounded the front row, ran around to the north aisle, and was going to run back up, when suddenly my feet went forward but my head stayed back. I suddenly remembered the string I had tied up. I hung myself on that darn string. I managed to keep my feet under me for the most part, but I wound up crashing into the third row of seats. The seats in the theatre are screwed down into a wooden floor. After I was done with my stunt, the first two seats of the third row were no longer screwed in. The crowd roared with laughter, my coworker spooks all roared with laughter, and now I had a repair job to do.

With a different movie every night, we didn't want to run the same gag with that witch every night because we were likely to have repeat customers. We all changed our costumes every night as well. We went all out and hog wild! That little witch sat up in the balcony all hooked up and ready to go for three nights without taking one shove down the string.

Thursday night came, and Steve and I decided it was time. I hadn't been upstairs all week after rigging this witch up. I remembered how I had laid it all out, and with Steve and the rest of the characters in place at the back of the theatre. I went up to let her fly, but when I got there, she was gone! Where did she go? Did she fly away? I found out later the witch was put to better use for the time being in the lobby, but I didn't know, and I didn't see her. I thought, "Damn, what do I do now?"

Aha! That stupid dummy was still sitting in his chair with a dumb look on his face watching the movie with a rope around his neck. I decided to rig him up fast. I picked him up and sat him on the banister of the balcony to tie him on the line. I had a little blanket that I also wanted to tie around him so he would hang down longer and maybe look like a ghost. So many plans and so little time. I was wrapping the blanket around the dummy's neck when *slip*, he slipped out of my hands and fell from the balcony to his untimely undoing. I think my heart skipped a beat, because this dummy was quite heavy, perhaps ten to fifteen pounds or so, and falling nearly twelve feet on an unsuspecting patron could really put a hurt on someone. He hit bottom, and it was quite a crash. He fell on the seat backs of one row and then crashed to the floor. Shrieks and screams could be heard caused by this very unusual noise. I looked down to see the damage, and luckily no one was sitting there. I breathed a sigh of relief. I threw the blanket from the balcony onto some unsuspecting patrons, and they looked like a bunch of cats in a feed sack trying to get out from underneath it with shrieks and screams. I was having fun now. I went downstairs, and Steve asked what the hell was going on. I explained the whole situation about the witch being gone and trying to hook up the dummy. He said he was standing in the aisle right next to where the dummy fell, and it scared the daylights out of him. He told me that at first he thought I fell from the balcony. I had scared Mr. Halloween, but that was the only time.

That dummy took quite a few dives off the balcony into the aisles after that. I'd toss him and Steve or one of our cohorts would jump scare some hapless victim who had just jumped from the dummy landing. But all good things must come to an end. The last time I threw him, his head popped off and went rolling down the aisle like a bowling ball down the lane. The head finally hit up against the third row, the opposite aisle from where I had broken the anchors. A rather large man was sitting in the aisle seat, and when that head hit his seat, he threw his arms back, gave out a whelp, leaned back, and broke all the anchors in that seat. Now both aisles' outer third row was screwed, or rather unscrewed. We kept the pieces of that dummy over the years, and he took a few headless dives, but he never quite did the trick like he did that first year. That blanket gave me a good idea. We had some black plastic camo netting, and I would roll it up and throw it out like a seine net trying to catch fish. It would sprawl out and cover four or five people. I laughed every time

I watched those folks flail away. They would wind up tearing it to shreds, however. Our crowd was mostly junior high kids and kids will be kids.

Christmas

We did basically the same thing at Christmas except the lobby was transformed into a gingerbread house and the room was made into something Christmas related. The best one is always Santa's workshop. Will and his wife, Amanda, are Santa and Mrs. Claus. Amanda seems to know every kid in town, and she can relay a name to Will quickly. Santa sits at his desk acting as if he is doing some heavy-duty naughty-and-nice list making. The kids' eyes get wide when they see Santa, but when Mrs. Claus let him know who was coming before they got there and Santa calls out their names, their mouths would virtually drop open. Santa knows and sees everything. The scene is truly heartwarming, and Will and Amanda play their roles perfectly.

After the show we place a couple of snow blowers on the balcony, and Santa sits in a chair outside with Mrs. Claus to his side with a basket of candy canes. The children line up for pictures and sit on his lap. It can last for quite a while. I get dressed up as Scrooge and bah humbug myself bored, but I'm not too busy that I can't watch what's going on. That first year I even shed a tear or two watching the kids enjoy the magic of Christmas. Another major attraction is the Grinch.

The Grinch is played by Paula. She does a wonderful job, not only entertaining but also making shy kids feel at ease. She lies on the ground, gets to their level, and high-fives them. Next thing you know, a shy kid that did not know what to think of this green thing suddenly is a new best friend. Before the movie starts, we spend some amount of time outside as customers walk up. Santa's chair is there sitting empty, but Paula will sit on her head with her legs straight up in the air. She does a fantastic job. I see her being the Grinch in our small town until she is physically unable to do so.

My outfit consists of a black suit jacket with tails and a fluffy old-fashioned type of tie. I wear a wig that is long and gray, glasses hanging off my nose, and a cane. Even with all this plus a surly attitude, calling kids street urchins or ragamuffins, the parents who know me can tell easily that it's me. One night Paula and I were outside early before showtime waiting for customers to come walking up, and I told her that she pisses me off. If I could have a costume where nobody knew who I was I could go hog wild. It's a good thing I don't have her costume because I can't imagine anyone, me or anyone else, doing a better job being the Grinch.

I still have lots of fun being Scrooge, but I'm not sure how entertaining it is to the kids. I will come into the auditorium very grumpy and pick out a child to sit next to. I'll make a mess eating my popcorn, asking the kid a bunch of questions like "What kind of job do you have?" or "Can you drive a truck?" or something along those lines. I eventually get on to them about making a mess with popcorn, even if they are not eating popcorn. They never do when I walk by them later and give them even more grief.

One night I walked around the front of the stage complaining aloud about something—usually I complain about why my movie is playing. It won all the awards for best picture ever! We had a sleigh up on the stage, and I stopped, grabbed a present, shook it, and acted as if I was listening to it rattle. One thing that you do not mess with is Christmas presents. This audience of kids let me have the business. I screamed, "Shut up and mind your business. It has my name on it." I took it to the side where a staircase up to an emergency exit was and threw it up the stairs. I walked away bah humbugging everyone. Eventually I came back down the aisle and sat down next to a kid, where I made a mess with popcorn and blamed it on him. About two rows up, a little girl, about five or six, was turned around and had her little eyes just over the seat back and was staring at me. I stared back. She finally said, "We went and got that present." I looked up at the sleigh and there it sat. Once again don't mess with Christmas presents around kids.

I have lots of fun doing this, but I'm not sure how entertaining it is to our customers. It's entertaining to me. My fellow board members who make up the backbone of how to make all this work, Deena, Angie, and Belinda, just put up with me. They go out of their way to allow me to amuse myself. They think I'm just a big kid, a little bigger than the ones who come in to see the shows. Maybe I am. My recent bout with brain cancer and coming face to face with the possibility of not having my normal life if I even survive at all has taught me to enjoy life a little more, share my talent, if you can call it that, a little more and just cut loose.

Rascal

Early in my "board-em," when producing different ways of raising revenue, I was given the opportunity to put on a play, a melodrama, or a reasonable facsimile thereof. In the span of a week or two, I wrote the melodrama. I had certain people in mind to play certain roles if they could manage the time that it took to put this on, and it took a lot of time. It was always a dream of mine to write a play and act on the stage again, and these people gave a lot of their spare time to make my dream happen. It was amateurish at best, but it was made with love.

I wound up playing the hero, Rascal P. Soultrane, but I was far from the star of the show. The real stars of the show were two of our board members, Angie and Belinda. They played a couple of local old ladies in town that would gossip and tell stories about actual folks in our town and the daily goings on. I put a lot of work and rewrites into their act. Even before rehearsals started, I could envision them getting the big laughs, and they did not disappoint. The cast and I got some chuckles and belly laughs; these gals brought it. They have a natural talent to make you laugh when you just stand around them and listen to them tell stories about what went on during their day in real life, so I knew that, with the right material, they could kill them, and they did. Deena, our other partner in crime, could do this as well. The three of them together could have the house howling if we had all three on the stage, but Deena got stuck doing all the tech work.

No matter what project we are working on, we always have fun, and you should hear some of the conversations that come out as a result of late nights getting ready for a program of some sort. It's not always G rated, but it's always funny. Even when someone is a little peeved about something and rants a little about what is bothering them, I am holding my laugher. These folks are funny, or I'm easily amused. There is no telling what may flow forth from someone's mouth.

Don't get me wrong—we have fun, but we are all business when it comes to the business of the theatre, and we do have our differences in opinion sometimes. The family atmosphere we have built over a few years has allowed us to not hold any grudges and to listen to and respect each other's concerns.

THE ENDING

I have had a wonderful life, and if it ended today, I would be a fulfilled man, but I hope it doesn't. I enjoy watching people, experiencing new things, and being entertained by you and everyone else. I suppose I also like to entertain you as well. If you know me and you are not in this book, don't think I have forgotten about you; you entertain me as well, but a book can only be so big. I have a million stories about ol' Suckass Benny, but I wanted to keep this book PG. The fun thing about him is that was his pet name for everyone, suckass. Once we got a new guy at work, Benny called him suckass like he did everybody else. This fellow told Benny that he didn't appreciate being called suckass and he would like for Benny to stop it. Benny apologized and stated he didn't intend to offend him. It's really a term of endearment if anything, but he said he would stop. The guy said thanks. As he was leaving, he said, "Goodbye, Benny." Benny replied, "Goodbye, Suckass."

There are many more stories like that about lots of people. I will continue to keep my eyes and ears open, and if you find me in your company, don't pay any attention to the fact that I am watching you from across the room. It is just little ol' me wondering what you may be thinking judging by the look on your face. Keep on entertaining me and I will try to keep on entertaining you.

ACKNOWLEDGMENTS

This book would not be possible without my lifelong partner in crime, my wife, Pam. She is the epitome of what marriage is supposed to be. A lot of folks don't seem to take the for better or worse, in sickness and in health stuff seriously. Pam always did, and she still does, and I do too. When I had one of my many surgeries, whether it was on a knee, shoulder, back, or brain, she always nursed me back to health. When I come up with a crazy idea such as to write a melodrama, audition for a play, or write a book, she may shake her head a little, but she allows me my whimsies no matter how big or small. I allow her hers as well, but hers are not nearly as huge as mine.

To my children, Melanie and Jennifer, my thanks for reminding me of the advice I always gave them: don't grow old and gray and say to yourself, "I wish I would've." I've gotten gray, but I haven't gotten old yet and I'm still doing the things before I do. I hope they are taking this advice now and after I'm gone as well as passing it on.

Thanks goes to my family and in particular my mother. Bone for bone we are the same. Every good thing inside of me comes from her. I've watched her work hard for me and my siblings' lives. She did without when we did with. Thanks go also to my dad. He left a strong work ethic for us that we all use to one extent or the other.

Thanks also go to all the friends I've had over all my years. Without some of their antics, this book would not be possible.

ABOUT THE AUTHOR

Felix Rainosek, a true Texan at heart, now resides in Kansas with his beautiful wife, a native Kansas farmer's daughter. Together, they have two children and four grandchildren. Felix, a skilled maintenance technician, has a passion for fixing things. He also has a deep love for the theater, enjoying both films and live performances. His knack for writing and performing in plays and melodramas is evident. His book, I Never Was A Cowboy, draws inspiration from the vibrant characters he's encountered in his life, offering a captivating read for all, especially those in their middle years.

Milton Keynes UK
Ingram Content Group UK Ltd.
UKHW020804130524
442628UK00004B/252

9 798822 948228